DIRECTOR'S CUT

NOTES ON BASICS OF FILM MAKING

VAIBHAV BIST

Dedicated to all budding Film Makers right there, everywhere !!

- VAIBHAV BIST

Contents

Foreword					vii

Preface					ix

Prologue					xi

FILM ELEMENTS

HOW TO WATCH AND ANALYSE A FILM

PRODUCTION AND BREAKDOWN

Quotes For All Film Enthusiasts					81

FOREWORD

Since my teenage, I have passion for film making, writing scripts, editing and acting, in short for complete film making process. I have grown up watching some marvellous films from all over the world. And yes ofcourse I love my Hindi films a lot. A self confessed fan of AAMIR KHAN and CHRISTOPHER NOLAN, I keep learning everday even when I make a film or do research on my subject for next film.

In this book, I have combined the notes that were made by me during my film making learning period, Circa 2009-2011.

ANY SINGLE DAY WHEN I AM NOT SHOOTING FILMS, I TAKE IT AS IF I AM KILLING MY TIME !!

I JUTS LOVE FILM MAKING.

Preface

THE FIRST AND FOREMOST DUTY OF A FILM MAKER IS TO EDUCATE YOURSELF !

OBSERVE THE WORLD AROUND YOU A LOT. YOU WILL SURELY GET A LOT OF STORIES THAT ARE YET TO BE TOLD !

- VAIBHAV BIST

PROLOGUE

In this book, you will find notes on basics of acting, film making and distribution. Also short notes on film analysis and relationship between cinema and society.

FILM ELEMENTS

FILM LANGUAGE

Film language, the most elegant language in creative world that has the power to pierce right through heart of it's reader(audience in actual). The language of using pictures, sound and editing to tell a story is called film language. Now this language has five elements that are called five elements of cinema- Literary design, Visual Design, Cinematography, Sound and Editing. Let's have a briefing of these elements.

LITERARY DESIGN

First of all you think of an idea. An idea that you want to culminate into a film. But how is that possible? Only through a well written script.

Write down basic idea of the plot you are thinking of making a film on. Now think of the genre you want to mold that plot into. There are several genres of scripts and films i.e. Romance, Thriller, Horror, Comedy, Action, Drama to name a few. After deciding upon a genre, you develop your final one liner of the story. This one liner will decide your full synopsis i.e. the story of the film.

After writing down the synopsis, you have to develop your script's treatment. A treatment is nothing but a dialogue-less, scene wise breakdown of your script's screenplay according to your story plotting. That is what actually is going on in each scene.

Examples of above mentioned things are as follows.

PLOT : A love story with a twist of a disease.

ONE LINER : A girl named Riya, age 28, is collecting old roses from different parts of her house that were given to her by Rohan, her college classmate, eight years ago. Each rose has a flashback of it's own with their love story ending in a twist.

SYNOPSIS : Here you can give detail of why actually Rohan is in love with Riya. What is the purpose of Rohan in giving those Roses to her and what exactly is happening in those flashbacks attached to each rose. What can be a twisted ending to this love story.

TREATMENT : SCENE WISE

SCENE 1 : IT CAN BE A COLLEGE SCENE FEATURING THE FIRST TIME ROHAN GIVES A ROSE TO RIYA.

SCENE 2 : SECOND TIME, HE GIVES HER A ROSE AGAIN.

AND SO ON.

The treatment of any script would depend upon your imagination and creativity. Ask yourself first of all that why I am working on such a script? Will this be feasible enough for me or for my producer monetarily? Will it be able to strike a chord with the audiences? Or will this provide me a creative and artistic satisfaction?

Further, please notice that no one on earth can teach you creativity. It will come to you naturally or through experience. Experience comes through knowledge. Knowledge will come through your own research. Read several topics, news, books on your selected topic/plot. Notice how a twist is given to that plot in those resources. Then think of your imagination about that plot and here it is! You will definitely get a good idea to move your script ahead in terms of screenplay.

Every screenplay can be classified into a three act structure.

First act – beginning of the story, establishing the characters.

Second act – middle of the story, producing a reason for the conflict within the story.

Third act – The climax. Giving a perfect end to the story.

3 C's of SCREENPLAY

There are many ways of constructing a plot. One I find useful is to consider what I call the three C's:

Conflict

Choice

Consequence

You can use these to develop your main plot and they are equally useful in constructing the smaller components of your story–the individual scenes. This is especially true in helping you construct the hardest part of any story, the middle or Act II.

You can use the three C's to come up with a log line, which also is the spine of your story. For example:

A young man obsessed with becoming a great drummer finds himself tested to the limit by a brilliant but abusive teacher.

The three C's don't always occur in the same order. In this instance, it's the young man's choice (to become a great drummer) that leads to the conflict (the harsh demands of the teacher) that leads to the consequence (being tested to the limit).

This order is typical of stories in which the protagonist sets out to achieve some kind of goal.

A scene can start with either a conflict or a choice that leads to one.

For example, let's say you're writing a thriller in which your protagonist's identity has been stolen. Fearful that this is leading to her being framed for a murder, she takes action to discover who is responsible.

She finds a clue that the woman impersonating her is going to be at a certain restaurant for dinner. She decides to confront her (the choice). At the restaurant, she challenges the woman (conflict). Unfortunately, the bad guys sent a ringer, and the protagonist is arrested for assault (consequence).

That leads to a new conflict, between her and the system. She has to make a new choice: insist on what seems like a crazy story, and risk being sent to a psychiatric hospital, or play along and accept the blame for something she didn't do.

Whichever choice she makes will have further consequences that lead to more conflict, until there is some kind of final showdown.

Building the strongest scene and story

In each scene we can ask what choices the protagonist has, and which one leads to the most interesting story development. Obviously, the choice has to be consistent with the character you have created, and the character and his or her choices are influenced by the genre as well as the plot.

In action stories, we tend to give the character very few options; in each new development he finds himself faced with some seemingly impossible task he must perform in order to avoid disaster. Think James Bond.

In more sophisticated stories, there are several viable options and which one the protagonist chooses helps us to understand him better and perhaps consider what we would do in his place. In that version, James Bond might stop to consider whether the outcome of the violent tasks being demanded of him are worth the sacrifice of his humanity. Confronted with a particularly vulnerable beautiful woman, he might opt *not* to sleep with her just to get the information he needs.

How this helps you with the middle of your story

The middle is where many stories weaken. They cease to grow and we feel like the story has been padded. This happens even though there is all kind of conflict and action.

The reason is that the protagonist has stopped making new choices. The story has set up the basic conflict, and if the escalation of the conflict is just mechanical, the story will stall in terms of its emotional impact.

To see how this works, let's go back to the woman whose identity has been stolen. In Act II they take all the money in her bank account, then they make it look like she's been embezzling money at work so she loses her job, then they set up a situation in which she's arrested for assault.

Those are all escalations, but if they are only the result of the actions of the people who are using her, they will not be as powerful as if they are at least in part the result of new choices she makes. For example, maybe she decides, 'If I'm going to be convicted for embezzling money whether or not I've done it, I might as well do it." Shortly after she's been fired, and with her bank account already cleaned out, she takes some of the company's money in order to be able to fight back against the people setting her up. She's made a moral choice that feels like an emotional escalation.

Even more dramatically, if she's going through a divorce and a custody battle, she might decide that in light of what's happening to her, her child would be safer with her ex-husband; although it tears her up, she drops her quest for custody. (Hmm, do we think the ex-husband might be in on all this?)

In short, the middle of your story will grow in intensity if the escalation operates on several levels, rather than just the degree of physical threat to your protagonist.

Some of the big action movies that lack this try to cover for it with bigger explosions and more impressive effects, but for audiences with an attention span longer than 30 seconds, this ploy can work for only so long.

Whether you use the three C's right from the start, or to help you strengthen your story once you've bashed out a first draft, giving thought to choices, conflicts, and consequences can help you write a more powerful screenplay.

ELEMENTS OF SCRIPTING

These are the unique margin, case, and position attributes that give feature film script text the format and consistency expected by all participants. Once you are accustomed to them you'll be able to tell your story the way an industry reader is accustomed to seeing it. The elements for a script are:

- Scene Heading
- Action
- Character Name
- Dialogue
- Parenthetical
- Extensions
- Transition
- Shot

A scene heading is basically the information you are giving to script reader about the place and time for the scene to be happened.

#1: EXT/AN OFFICE/DAY or INT/AN OFFICE/NIGHT

#1 stands for SCENE 1. EXT and INT stands for whether the scene is happening exterior or interior of the place mentioned. Office is an example of where location name is to be fixed and DAY-NIGHT are the time effect of the scene.

If the next scene happens in the same day or night, the scene gets the heading ending as DAY CONTINUOUS or NIGHT CONTINUOUS.

Action is what exactly your characters are doing in that particular scene. For example,

#1: EXT/AN OFFICE/DAY

John is sitting in his office cabin and doing some typing work while sipping in coffee. He is looking a bit worried. (ACTION)

Next comes the Character's name and his/her dialogue after the action. Example,

#1: EXT/AN OFFICE/DAY

John is sitting in his office cabin and doing some typing work while sipping in coffee. He is looking a bit worried. He call in peon by ringing his desk bell. The peon steps in his cabin.

JOHN

Please get me some sugar !

PEON

(with a smile)

Definitely sir.

Now in this scene, the words within the brackets " (with a smile) " form the Parenthetical part. That is whether the character is speaking or doing something while weeping, smiling or any other emotion or body language.

Now we come to Extension . An extension is a technical note placed directly to the right of the Character name that denotes how the character's voice will be heard by the audience. An Off-Screen voice can be heard from a character out of the camera range, or from another room altogether. For example, if in the same above mentioned scene, we are seeing John inside his cabin and we hear Peon's voice from outside of obeying John's order for bringing him some sugar. The same case applies also if there is a VOICE OVER in any scene.

After this scene if we want to jump on to the next scene, we insert some Transition, i.e. CUT TO or MATCH DISSOLVES , etc.

#1: EXT/AN OFFICE/DAY

John is sitting in his office cabin and doing some typing work while sipping in coffee. He is looking a bit worried. He call in peon by ringing his desk bell. The peon steps in his cabin.

JOHN

Please get me some sugar !

PEON

(with a smile)

Definitely sir.

CUT TO...

#2: EXT/A MARKET PLACE/ DAY CONT.

Now we come to the last element of scripting that is a shot. While writing a screenplay, it's a writer's choice whether to break the scenes down more deeply into shots also. As it can be done later in pre production part by the direction team as well.

So that's how one can write a screenplay by following above mentioned points in literary design.

VISUAL DESIGN : MISE EN SCENE

Visual design basically deals with how visually appealing you make your scene while filming. Here one important term can be used named as Mise–en-scene.

Mise-en-scene, a French term meaning "place on stage," refers to all the visual elements of a theatrical production within the space provided by the stage itself. Film makers have borrowed the term and have extended the meaning to suggest the control the director has over the visual elements within the film image. Four aspects of mise-en-scene which overlap the physical art of the theatre are **setting, costume, lighting and movement of figures.** Control of these elements provides the director an opportunity to stage events. Using these elements, the film director stages the event for the camera to provide his audience with vivid, sharp memories. Directors and film scholars alike recognize mise-en-scene as an essential part of the director's creative art.

Setting, as an important visual element of film, includes all that the viewer sees which informs time and place apart from costume. This aspect of mise-en-scene plays an extremely active role in film and periodically may assume as much importance in the total film as the action, or events. Drama on screen, for example, may not even require actors if swirling desert sand, wildly lashing palm fronds, or a falling autumn leaf dynamically contribute to dramatic effect. Although setting provides a container for dramatic action, its significance goes beyond that and invites the film maker to control its various aspects artistically. One method of setting control lies in selection of natural or artificial locale. Lush green countryside, barren mountain plain, tropical jungle, rocky seashore or snowy forest suggest a story line as well as conflict that is very different from Gothic cathedral, inner-city ghetto, thatched cottage or sterile institution. The selection process includes, too, the choice of constructing the set rather than using an already existing locale. Control may be extended, then, to determination of historical authenticity or creative blends intended to add to the text's meaning. The set, in other words, might represent exactly a particular place, or it might be deliberately constructed to include the possible, improbable or even impossible locale. For instance, tilted buildings with minute windows and slanted doors might be constructed ingeniously to orient viewers to a world wherein ideas can be expected to differ from their own. Whether selected or constructed, real or surreal, setting functions variously to orient viewers, to contribute dramatic impact, and to add meaning to the film's narrative. Setting's ability to add meaning to narrative implies that props—part of the setting given specific significance in the total action—are also part of the control directors dictate in film art. A bottle of prescription medicine with a name, a shattered window pane, a broken heel, or a shower curtain shown early in a film may appear later to provide emphasis or even real causal relationships between otherwise seemingly coincidental events. The bottle of medicine is used, for instance, to kill the very patient who seeks good health. Or, the shower curtain hides a killer who later wraps his victim's body in it. Selecting, constructing, and arranging elements of setting all give the director powerful control over his art. Staging the event for the camera, the director exhibits craft and creativity as he uses this aspect of mise-en-scene.

Costume, or clothing and its accessories, is also an important visual element in film. Directors concerned with verisimilitude (historical reality) often go to great lengths to research clothing style, textile, and dye likely to be used by folk of a certain era, for costume is an indispensable means of establishing authenticity. Costume as an aspect of mise-en-scene in film, however, gains even more significance when directors manipulate costume so that it functions in special ways in the film as a whole. Costume can serve to enhance the narrative, or story, for instance, by suggesting social position of characters. Obviously a threadbare cotton shirt gives a very different picture than does a silk designer gown. Costume can imply, too, psychological disposition of characters. Viewers certainly gain very different insights into characters wearing casual shoes, loosely fitting jeans with blouses as opposed to those clad in skin tight leathers and wearing stiletto heels.

Costume also can hint at character development in the film. When an innocent normally dressed in pale frocks switches to siren red, the audience recognizes a gain in experience. Thus, costume becomes a special tool in the director's kit. In addition to informing narrative through contribution to setting, character, and plot, clothing—as an aspect of mise-en-scene—functions also as a prop upon which the film's unity may rest. Any portion of a costume may become a prop. Dracula's cape, for instance, tells viewers more and more as first it suggests concealment of evil and later provides a vehicle for the victim's entrapment. Likewise, the cross pendant in an initial shot seems merely a part of costume until other deliberate shots of that prop allow the viewer to pull the story's thread tighter. The pendant, the viewer learns, houses a secret necessary for the conflict's resolution. Anything—sunglasses, a six-gun, a cane, or a pipe—may be a prop derived from costume. The prop becomes significant in the ongoing action of the film. The prop's reoccurrence contributes to viewer's application of the total film. And, it is the director's selection and arrangement of costume as an aspect of mise-en-scene gives him control of visual elements necessary to effective filming. Figure Behavior Like setting and costume, figure expression and movement are important elements of mise-en-scene used by the director to support the narrative as well as help develop the thematic unity of a film. Figure expression refers to the facial expressions and the posture of an actor, whereas figure movement refers to all other actions of the actor, including gestures. Two of the most important aspects of film study are appropriateness of the expression of the actors and the control the director exhibits over the actor's movements. Often, viewers tend to think of actors as representing real people and, therefore, underestimate the art required in direction. The filmgoer must keep in mind that the actors' behavior on the screen is carefully controlled by the director. The director causes the actors to behave in a way that supports a particular thematic element of the film. A scene like the following illustrates this type of control: A man whom the mob intends to kill visits his lover for the last time before fleeing the country. The scene takes place in a small cabin. The cabin has one entrance next to a large window on the front wall. Two additional rooms are adjacent to the main living area where the man and his lover sit on the couch. They are engaged in animated conversation. Disturbed by the discussion, the woman gets up and moves toward the large window at the front of the room. Immediately upon being framed by the window, she is shot. Analysis of the woman's movement from the couch to the window allows the film student to begin to understand the director's control over figures in a film. Here, it is not by accident or by some independent motive of the character that this particular movement takes place. In part, it is the director's knowledge of the significance of the woman's being shot instead of the man which causes him to direct the woman to the window rather than, say, to the kitchen. Likewise, the man's witnessing of the woman's murder reinforces the importance of her movement to the window (the place providing opportunity for her murder). The director's control over movement gives him more artistic power as he deals with the narrative demands of the script. Figure expression, as an element of mise-en-scene, also provides artistic power to the director. Because the actors in a film are used as vehicles of expression by the director, the viewer must keep in mind that an actor's performance should be examined in terms of how well it complements the film's message as opposed to how well the actor's performance supports the viewer's conception of behavior in the real world. The viewer's preconceived notions of "realistic" behavior should not interfere with his understanding of the appropriateness of the expressions of the actors. The appropriateness of an actor's expressions ought to be judged according to that particular actor's behavior within a particular environment. A character's pattern of behavior can alert the viewer to the appropriateness or inappropriateness of an actor's expression. If a character exhibits an expression which is opposed to the expressions he has been displaying throughout the film, the viewer might be led to believe that the actor is demonstrating inappropriate behavior. A scene like the following shows the importance of appropriate behavior: A heroine in a film demonstrates that she is always under complete emotional control in the face of crisis. Near the end of the film, the character is thrust into a situation less critical to her emotional well-being than several earlier events. In the midst of this trying but not critical situation, the actress displays an exaggerated facial expression. The viewer may feel as he watches that the actress's expression is not consistent with the previously exhibited pattern of behavior. He is likely to conclude that the expression of the actress is inappropriate to the character she is portraying in the film. However, if the heroine appears from the beginning of the film as someone who is emotionally unstable, an extreme facial expression might be accepted by the viewer as appropriate even if that behavior had not been exhibited by the character earlier in the film. The expression of the actress could be considered generally inappropriate. Within the context of the character's pattern of behavior, however, this extreme expression is appropriate to the heroine's emotional makeup. The viewer should always remember that the appropriateness or inappropriateness of a character's behavior should be judged in relation to the setting of the particular scene and the overall make-up of that particular character.

Lighting - To the film director, lighting is more than illumination that enables the viewer to see the action. Lighting, like the other aspects of mise-en-scene, is a tool used by the director to convey special meaning about a character or the narrative to the viewer. Lighting can help define the setting of a scene or accentuate the behavior of the figures in the film. The quality of lighting in a scene can be achieved by manipulating the quality and the direction of the light. When the director manipulates the quality of the lighting, or the relative intensity of the illumination, he can control the impact of the setting or the figure behavior has on the viewer. By using lighting that creates clearly defined shadows, the director can suggest a strong division between two spatial areas of a scene. For example, if the setting contains a definite area of shadow, it would be easy for the director to create a feeling of suspense by having one of the figures in the film move into the shadows. In this scene not only does the mood of the setting become intense, but the behavior of the figure may seem exaggerated. Whereas hard lighting creates crisp edges around images and between spatial areas of the scene, soft lighting produces a diffused illumination. If the director is concerned with emphasizing a source of confusion for a character or the lack of clarity of a particular element of the narrative, he will usually use lighting that tends to blur contours and textures of objects in order to stress the lack of contrast between two extreme locations or postures. Take, for example, two characters, one good and one evil, portrayed in a scene in which the director has chosen to use soft lighting. In this scene the director can send the viewer two messages about the relationship between good and evil in his film. By eliminating the crisp edges of shadow and light, the director may suggest that distinguishing between good and evil people is not an easy task in the view of the world presented in his film. Likewise, the director may suggest that situations as well as people may be difficult or impossible to analyze in terms of all good or all evil. At any rate, it is important to keep in mind that hard and soft are relative terms which designate two extreme conditions of illumination. Actually, most lighting arrangements are variations of hard or soft lighting. When the director concerns himself with the path of light from the source to the object illuminated, he controls the direction of the light. A carefully controlled direction of lighting allows the director to set the mood of a particular scene.

There are five primary types of directional lighting: frontal lighting, side lighting, back lighting, under lighting, and top lighting. Frontal lighting is used when the director wants to eliminate shadows from a scene. It is especially useful when a scene takes place outdoors at high noon or in an indoor location such as a business office. Side lighting is often used when the features of a character or an object play an important role in the development of the narrative. Sidelight causes the features of an object to cast sharp shadows. A director might use sidelight to emphasize the shadows cast by the lips of a character who has been revealed as a habitual liar. Back lighting illuminates only the edges of an object. This type of lighting is used when a silhouette effect is desired. For instance, if a director wishes to conceal the identity of a particular character in a scene, he backlights the figure to allow the viewer to see only the outline of the character's body. Under lighting comes from below the object and tends to distort the features and shape of the object. If the viewer is shown a haunted house in a film, the director probably used under lighting to create the eerie image used in the scene. Top lighting, lighting which shines from directly above the object, can be used to direct the viewer's attention toward an area above the objects in the scene. Take, for example, a character in a film who is lost in the desert. The director could use toplight in the film to stress the deadly effects of the blazing sun on this hopelessly lost individual. Though any of the directional types of lighting can be used alone in a scene, two or more types may be used in combination to create a special effect.

Though each element of mise-en-scene is combined with other elements to create a specific atmosphere in every film, studying elements of mise-en-scene separately helps the viewer understand the function of each particular element. By focusing on the setting of a scene, the viewer can identify the exact importance of the time and place that he is shown so that he can think about the scene in relationship to the proper historical or cultural context. Costume, like setting, helps the viewer understand the action of a scene in relation to a larger context. It also allows the director to develop important character traits in his characters. Concentrating on the behavior of the figures helps the viewer to understand the personal motivation of the individual characters. Careful observation of figure behavior also allows the viewer to understand the role of each character in relation to the development of the story. When attempting to understand the mood of a scene, the viewer should always remember to pay close attention to the lighting. Lighting can intensify or subdue a setting, but regardless of its effect lighting is one more tool that the director uses to complete his cinematic statement. Therefore, lighting should be a vital concern to the student of film. By studying each of these elements as separate entities the student of film can begin to understand the important role that the manipulation of the elements of mise-en-scene plays within the entire context of film. And, by studying these elements as separate entities, the student of film can begin to appreciate the artistry required in film making.

FRAMING (MOVEMENT OF FIGURES) Onscreen / Offscreen Space (an image that is contained within the borders of the screen/a suggested image that is left to be imagined by the viewer—what the listener (not visually projected) is doing while the speaker (projected onto the screen) in a telephone conversation talks into the phone. The image created when the sound of a crash is heard but the crash is not seen. Angle Relationship of the camera to the subject High=weak, subordinated, controlled (when not used for maximum wideness—to show mass or crowd size instead of weakness) Low=strong, subordinating, controlling Flat=value neutral; neither controlling nor controlled; factual, etc relative value when juxtaposed to other angles: stronger than high angle and weaker than low angle Tilt angle=when the camera angle is other than 90 degrees may suggest character, action, conclusions, suspicions are not "right" (as in right angled); perhaps not being presented accurately, or intended as stated within the context of the action, etc Framing—Shot Distances [the closer the subject, the more potent, powerful, able to create change; the farther away, the less potent, the weaker, less able to create change]

1. Extreme long shot: A panoramic view of an exterior location, photographed from a great distance, often as far as a quarter mile away–sometimes an establishing shot that sets context for later closer shots.

2. Long shot: A broad view of objects or action of principle interest. This shot allows general recognition of the subject at the expense of detail. Also used as an establishing shot. Reveals the human full human figure, though more in the middle- than fore- or background. (View from audience to proscenium arch)

3. Medium shot: A relatively close shot, usually revealing the human figure from head to knees, feet to navel (bellybutton).

4. Medium Close up: A relatively close shot, usually revealing the human from head to waist, feet to thighs, or knees to navel (bellybutton).

5. Close up: Reveals head and shoulder of human figure in central focus of frame.

6. Extreme Close up: Reveals a body part: a face, an eye, a pupil; a finger, a fingernail, etc.

CINEMATOGRAPHY & EDITING

Cinematography is the art of motion-picture photography and filming either electronically by means of an image sensor, or chemically by means of a light-sensitive material such as film stock.

Cinematographers use a lens to focus reflected light from objects into a real image that is transferred to some image sensor or light-sensitive material inside a movie camera. These exposures are created sequentially and preserved for later processing and viewing as a motion picture. Capturing images with an electronic image sensor produces an electrical charge for each pixel in the image, which is electronically processed and stored in a video file for subsequent processing or display. Images captured with photographic emulsion result in a series of invisible latent images on the film stock, which are chemically "developed" into a visible image. The images on the film stock are projected for viewing the motion picture.

It includes: Camera angles, camera movements, shot sizes, lighting, composition.

While a basic introduction has been given above for the same, we will now move to a more briefing into cinematography.

The HUMAN EYE scans pictures from left to right.

HORIZONTAL LINES – Move from left to right
VERTICAL LINES – Move from top to bottom
DIAGONAL OR OBLIQUE LINES tend to sweep upward
TERRITORIAL SPACE – movie images must tell a story in time. A story that involves human beings and their problems.

THREE VISUAL PLACES – MIDGROUND, FOREGROUND, BACKGROUND

SPACE is one of the principal mediums of communication in film

Dominant characters:

- Always given more space to occupy than others are.
- You can define, adjust and redefine human relationships by exploiting spatial conventions.

PROXEMIC PATTERNS – Climax, noise level and the degree of light all tend to alter the space between individuals

INTIMATE:

- Eighteen inches away.
- Distance of LOVE,
- COMFORT,
- TENDERNESS between individuals.

PERSONAL:

- Eighteen inches to about four feet away.
- Reserved for friends and acquaintances.

SOCIAL: Four feet to about twelve feet away.

- Business and
- Casual social gatherings.

PUBLIC:

- Twelve to about twenty feet away.

BASICS OF FOCAL LENGTH

Forget the technical definition of focal length, it's unnecessary to understand it or practice cinematography.

The Angle of View

Lenses cut out parts of what's in front of you, and only show a portion of it. You can actually measure the angle of it from the position of the camera, and you have what is called the angle of view.

Want to get a tighter shot? There are two ways. You can either walk closer, or you can get a different lens with a smaller angle of view.

It's important to pick the right camera, depending on where and what you're shooting. When it comes to sensor sizes, there are *full-frame* and *crop* sensors.

A full-frame sensor will give you a wider angle of view for the same lens, while a crop sensor will give you a tighter angle of view.

Full-frame vs Crop Cameras

Full-frame cameras have a sensor which is in the same dimensions as a 35mm film format. This is consider to be a standard, due to its long usage as a uniform format for production from the early 20th century. The focal lengths of lenses are based on this 35mm standard.

But, if you're using a camera with a crop sensor, the focal length of the lens will not determine your angle of view. What a crop camera does is what its name implies – it crops out a part of the image from what you would usually see on a full-frame camera. A crop sensor is any kind of sensor which is smaller than the 35mm standard. The common types of crop sensors are the APS-C and micro 4/3 systems.

In order to know the angle of view or focal length with a crop sensor, you can measure it by the focal length multiplier.

Crop Factor

Crop factor on camera sensors changes depending on the manufacturer of the camera. For example, the crop factor of a Canon APS-C camera is 1.6x.

What does that mean?

The image will look different if you're using a 50mm lens on a Canon 5D, a full-frame sensor camera, or on a Canon 70D, an APS-C crop sensor camera. On the Canon 5D, you will get an image you expect from a 50mm lens. But, with a Canon 70D the focal length of the lens is multiplied with the crop factor (50×1.6), resulting in a focal length or angle of view of 80mm. If you would put a 35mm lens on the Canon 70D, you would roughly get a look of a 50mm on a full-frame camera.

The quality of your image is directly influenced by the quality of your sensor.

There has been a long and bloody debate about sensor sizes and the advantages of full-frame over crop sensor cameras. Full-frame cameras do over-perform in two things, which are more limiting on crop sensor cameras – they are better in low-light settings and they will get you a shallower depth of field. Apart from that, you could say that it doesn't matter if you have a full-frame or a crop sensor camera – as long as you know what you're doing and what you want from your image.

The number we give lenses to represent the angle of view, is the focal length. It does have a technical definition as well, but that definition is in no way useful to cinematographers. If you want to know what it is, wikipedia is a good place. For those who don't want to waste time on unnecessary theory, all you have to know is the angle of view is always, always dependent on the size of the sensor.

A larger sensor will give you a wider angle of view for the same lens, while a smaller sensor will give you a tighter angle of view.

Since sensor sizes are all over the place nowadays, if you put the same lens on different cameras, you might get different angles of view. A Sony a7S II will be different from the Panasonic GH5 will be different from a Red Raven will be different from an Arri Alexa, because their sensor lengths are all different.

So what we really need is a gold standard. Some starting point from which to calculate the rest if we ever need to. I've written an extensive article on the 35mm equivalent and crop factors if you want to learn more, I've decided the 35mm full frame format is the best gold standard we have today. It's been around long enough and is most relevant for cinematography. By 35mm full frame I'm talking about 135 or a sensor measuring exactly 36mm x 24mm. The Nikon D4, D850, Sony a7S II, a7R III and so on are all full frame sensors.

Wide Angle, Normal and Telephoto

We can also differentiate between the types of lenses based on the different focal lengths they provide. Depending on this, all of them can be used to shape the image and enhance the narrative of the film.

Ultra wide-angle lens – focal length between 8mm and 24mm

These are extremely wide lenses, allowing you to capture almost 180 degrees around the lens. If the focal length is up to 14mm these lenses are called fisheye lenses. Due to their wide viewing area, they create visible distortions in the image. For that reason, fisheye lenses are almost never used in film.

Wide-angle lens – focal length between 24mm and 35mm

Wide angle lenses have a small focal length and a wide angle of view. In film, they are great for master shots, as they include all of the information of a wider space with very little distortion. If you use a wide-angle lens, you can also approach a subject without excluding the background information. But, careful not to approach too close the subject with a wide-angle lens, as you will create distortions in the image.

Standard/normal lens – focal length between 35mm and 70mm

A standard/normal lens produces an image which roughly matches what we see with our eyes. The best equivalent of this is the 50mm lens, which is one of the most versatile and used lenses. They create almost no distortions, making them perfect for portraits of subjects.

Telephoto lens – focal length between 70mm and 300mm (or more)

Telephoto lenses can be characterized as lenses which have a focal length bigger than the physical size of the lens. They are sometimes mistaken for zoom-lenses, even though they don't necessarily need to be a zoom lens. They come in a range of focal lengths, from *medium-telephoto* (from 67mm to 206mm) and *super-telephoto* (over 300mm). They are great for isolating your subject from the background, but should be handled on a tripod due to their size. It becomes hard to track a subject with these lenses, since the slightest shake of the lens is visible in the image. But, if you can make your movement smooth and not too fast, zoom lenses can also become a valuable tool.

So let's say I want a wide angle of view. To get that I use what is very loosely called a wide angle lens. Let's just say we're using a 24mm lens for this example. What's this "24mm"? It's just a name. It's not 24 degrees, but it represents a certain angle of view on a 35mm full frame sensor, and we call it wide angle, through tradition.

Focal lengths are written as XXmm, where XX is a number (single digit to as high as four digits)

Any number smaller than this is wider. So the wider you need to go, the smaller this number gets. It's always in millimeters and is written on the front and sides of your lenses. This number is called the focal length.

The higher the number, the smaller the angle of view. Of course, this is only true if you're using the same sensor for comparison. E.g., a 24mm lens on a full frame camera is wide, but the same lens on a Micro Four Thirds sensor would be the equivalent to a 48mm lens. If this is confusing to you, then please read my article on the crop factor and the 35mm equivalent. Now here's the thing, a 48mm is not considered wide. In fact, in the full frame world, a 50mm lens is considered normal, by tradition.

So we have a range of lenses that go from super wide to wide angle. Through tradition, wides roughly end at about 35mm. From 35mm to about 70mm we have the normal range. And finally, anything above 70mm could be considered telephoto. When it goes beyond 200mm, people also call it super-telephoto. Beyond 2000mm, you're looking at a telescope.

If you want to shoot a wide vista, say the grand canyon, you might love the ultra wide angle focal lengths. If you want to shoot mid shots or documentary-style, you might like the normal range, if you want to flatter your star, then pick a telephoto lens.

So the important things you need to know about focal lengths

1. Focal lengths by itself don't really mean anything. You also need to know the size of the sensor it's going to be used for.
2. The smaller the number the wider it gets and more spacious everything looks. The larger the number the tighter it gets and more compressed or restricted everything looks.
3. Most important. Different focal lengths tell a story differently. The entire emotional impact changes for the same sized shot with different focal lenses, so choosing the right focal length is hugely a matter of personal taste.

How do you know which one you should pick?

Here's a simple trick. Have you clicked photos or shot videos? Go back to all the photos you have clicked, or footage u have shot and see if you've cropped them mostly. If you've cropped most of your photos/videos then you probably are not a wide-angle person. On the other hand, do you feel most motivated with a wide angle lens? Then maybe that's the focal length range you should start out with.

The traditional range runs like this:

14mm is ultra wide.

24mm is wide.

35mm is between normal and wide, and many consider this to be close to what the eye sees.

50mm is normal, which means the face is not distorted, and it gives you the most unbiased look, if you will.

85mm is portrait, and flatters your subject. Telephoto distorts the other way, makes faces look thinner. Anything more will flatter them even more, but you are hit with the practical limits of space in cinematography. You have to move further back but there might not be room.

If you need to shoot wildlife or birds, then go telephoto or even super-telephoto.

Primes or Zooms?

If you know exactly what you want, then you can work with prime lenses.

Prime lenses are lenses with just one focal length. If you know you like a range, say normal range, then pick a zoom lens in that range. That's why you see most camera companies have three main zooms – 16-35mm, which is the wide range, 24-70mm, the normal range, and 70-200mm, the telephoto range. See? Other people have already done the thinking for you.

Prime lenses are preferred by cinematographers because of the image quality they produce and the speed of the lens. Since they have fewer glass elements within their construction, the light is less distorted once it reaches the sensor. This results in a clearer and sharper image.

The speed of the lens is determined by the aperture (f/stop); with a lower f/stop you can shoot in lower light setting and use a faster shutter speed. For example, prime lenses with a f/1,8 or f/1,4 are highly desired.

Zoom lenses have a different range of focal lengths, due to their more complex construction. The focal length on zoom lenses can be changed by turning the zoom ring on the lens. For that reason zoom lenses are usually more difficult to produce and they are consequently more expensive than prime lenses.

If you know you like a range, say normal range, then pick a zoom lens in that range. That's why you see most camera companies have three main zooms – 16-35mm, which is the wide range, 24-70mm, the normal range, and 70-200mm, the telephoto range. See? Other people have already done the thinking for you.

Zoom lenses can be a great asset if you're on a tight shooting schedule and you cannot afford to waste time changing lenses. You can just change your focal length on the zoom ring, within the range of your lens. Also, zoom lenses are usually not as fast as prime lenses. If you're thinking of buying a quality, fast zoom lens, be prepared to invest more money.

Focal Length and Film Directors

One amongst many decisions which directors have to continuously make during the shooting is the focal length of each shot. In most cases, this is a mutual decision between the director and the cinematographer.

Focal length directly establishes two crucial points: what is in the frame of the image and the depth of the image (or the 3-dimensional space of the image).

Directors use focus length and lenses to create a personal style – a fingerprint of their filmmaking language.

Director's Viewfinder

We all have an image in our head of a film director holding his hands up, trying to establish the framing of the image with his fingers. This is an old technique and it's rarely used today.

Instead, you can sometimes see a director walking around with a little gadget hanging around the neck. This is called the director's viewfinder. It's used by directors or cinematographers to determine the framing of the image, or in other words – the focal length needed for the shot.

Everybody uses a viewfinder in their own way. For some it's helpful during the shooting, while others prefer it during the pre-production phase, when they're location scouting and planning the shoot.

Either way, if your budget allows it, the director's viewfinder can be a helpful tool. In recent years, a more affordable option appeared – software-based viewfinders. They are available on smart phones and are considerably cheaper than a traditional director's viewfinder. Some directors prefer to rely on their directors of photography, leaving the camera-related decisions to them. Needless to say, the trust between a director and DP is crucial.

But as we learned from previously mentioned examples; it's equally important for a director to understand how focal length and lens choice, along with other important choices, build the character of the film. The right question to ask about focal lengths is: How do *you* see the world? I bet a focal length already exists that will make that come true.

EXPOSURE TRIANGLE

The "Exposure Triangle," as it is often referred to, is a handy way of interpreting the major components involved in the process of capturing an image.

It can be very overwhelming the first time you grab a hold of a camera. ISO settings, aperture and shutter speed, exposure compensation. Plus a million little buttons and switches with detailed menus and complex navigation.

Photography-for-beginners-_exposure-triangle.png

There are three main elements in the Exposure Triangle, which just so happen to be the three most primary camera settings you will need to address as you begin down your path to well-exposed shots. They are:

- Aperture
- Shutter Speed
- ISO

We will begin by breaking down each of these items to discuss what each one does, and how it's affecting your final image, before moving on to discuss how you should tackle setting up your shots.

Aperture

At the top of the Exposure Triangle sits aperture, most likely because of how big of an impact this setting will have on the overall aesthetic of your work.

Simply put, aperture refers to the specific setting of your lens' iris.

Iris

The iris is a mechanical, multi-bladed device inside of a camera lens that controls the amount of light that is allowed through to the camera's sensor behind it. Much in the way the human eye works, the iris can open to allow more light to enter the lens. Likewise, it can also restrict to reduce the amount of light.

While it may seem like an easy answer to adjust the exposure of a shot is to simply swing the aperture dial open and closed, the iris setting is not just controlling the amount of light passing through the lens. The aperture of a lens also affects its depth-of-field.

Depth-of-Field

The term refers to the plane of focus you will have to work within your shot.

- A wider aperture provides a more shallow depth-of-field, rending soft backgrounds that really separate and draw attention to your subject.
- A smaller aperture creates a greater depth-of-field, allowing more of a scene to be brought into the field of focus.

Because the aperture setting has such a huge impact on the look of your image, you don't really want to use this as much to control the amount of light coming into the camera, it's better to think of it as using the aperture to set the depth-of-field, knowing the impact it will have on your overall exposure.

What does shutter speed do?

It actually does what it sounds like; it controls the speed of how quickly the shutter will open and close for each exposure.

Often times, we see this number represented as a fraction of a second, something like 1/60. This comes from the photography world and refers to the physical opening and closing of the mechanical shutter, the opening of which is the inciting incident to creating an exposure, and allows light to strike the film or sensor and begin writing its image.

In the cinema world, more traditionally you'll often find a number represented as a degree, as in 180°.

Although it may sound illogical to refer to time as a degree, the reasoning for this has to do with the way that the mechanical shutters were produced for use in motion picture cameras. The shutter mechanisms themselves were essentially a spinning disk, actually more like a half-circle, and the speed which that disk would spin controlled how long each piece of film would be exposed before advancing to the next frame.

How Shutter Speed Affects Images

Because shutter speed has an effect on the amount of time each frame is exposed, it also ends up affecting the characteristics of motion. Allow me to explain by offering the extremes:

- A fast shutter speed setting, something like 1/250 or 45°, results in each frame having much sharper detail, but also more staccato, jumpy movement.
- A slow shutter speed, something like 1/24 or 360°, results in very smooth and fluid movement, but also tends to blur details unless both the camera and the subject remain perfectly still.

The goal of finding a correct shutter speed is to ensure that motion is represented accurately and looks similar to the way that we see with our eyes. While we can deviate from this "normal" shutter speed for effect, like creating tension during a fight scene by speeding up the shutter speed, most of our work will be shot with one shutter speed. Finding this normal setting depends on the frame rate that you are shooting, but thankfully, there is a handy way to figure out the speed you should be using.

How to Calculate Shutter Speed

When using shutter speed, the correct number can be found by doubling whatever your frame rate is. So, for example, if you are shooting at 24fps, your shutter should be set at 1/48. Sometimes you may run into an issue where your camera limits your options and you can't choose the exact setting you need, so you just have to use the closest position. (i.e. if you don't have a setting for 1/48, 1/50 will work just fine.)

Shutter angle makes this even easier and is the reason many camera operators use it. Since shutter angle is relative to your frame rate, the correct setting is always 180°.

Sometimes your normal setting can cause lighting in a scene to flicker. This can often be overcome by adjusting your shutter speed until it goes away. Some cameras feature a setting where you can adjust the shutter setting by hertz (Hz) for this very reason, as it is an extremely fine-grained tool you can use to help eliminate those annoying flickers.

What does ISO mean?

The final point on our exposure triangle is ISO, which refers to your camera's sensitivity to light.

ISO actually used to refer to the film stock's sensitivity to light, so a low ISO vs. a high ISO would scale as low sensitivity to light and high sensitivity to light. How does ISO work?

ISO 800 would be, for example, higher, and it would be a film stock one would choose to shoot in low light, because you'd need your film to have a higher sensitivity to the light available.

What else happens in this instance? The final image has more grain.

So to recap, in the film world, your ISO is selected based on the type of film you load into your camera. This makes ISO a much more limited part of balancing the exposure triangle when working with film. Shooting digitally, however, makes adjusting the ISO as easy as spinning a dial, but it's important to know the implications involved in your chosen setting.

How to Choose ISO

Choosing the best setting is very dependent on not only the camera model, but also the picture profile or specific camera settings you are using. On most stills cameras, conventional wisdom says to always use as low of an ISO as you can, in order to produce as clean of an image as possible, because, generally speaking, lower ISO settings have cleaner images with less noise or grain, while higher ISOs tend to trade off increased sensitivity for increased noise.

While this may work when starting out using standard or Rec. 709 picture profiles, it always pays to double-check your camera's manual or any white papers provided by the manufacturer. This is particularly important if you use any of the various Log options afforded by today's popular cameras, where your ISO settings can be much more limited and adjustments can have large effects on your dynamic range.

The best way to really learn how these adjustments affect your image is to shoot tests and review how they'll look and work in post.

The Exposure... Polygon ?

Once you've nailed the concepts behind the three points of the Exposure Triangle, finding a correct exposure by balancing the various options will become much easier. It is important to note that these three settings alone aren't the only thing influencing your exposure. The triangle is essentially an aperture shutter speed ISO chart. But there are ever MORE factors to consider!

The Fourth Point: Frame Rate

The unofficial fourth point of the exposure polygon is actually your frame rate. As your frame rate increases, your shutter speed will have to follow along. Each frame will then be exposed for less time, resulting in a darker exposure. While this may not show much a difference between 24p and 30p, start to get up to 60p or even 120p and you've begun to lose multiple stops of light and it will definitely be evident.

FILTERS FOR LENS

If you ask most consumer-camera owners why they keep a **filter** on their lens, a majority will most likely reply, "For protection." Although filters do, in fact, protect the surface of your lens against dust, moisture and the occasional thumb print, the primary function of lens filters is really to improve the image quality of the pictures you take—depending on the filter you're using and how you use it—in a variety of obvious and not-so-obvious ways.

The most basic filters are ultra-violet reducing filters (UV), Skylight filters and protection filters, which depending on the manufacturer are either glass filters with basic anti-reflective coatings, or in some cases, merely plainclothes UV filters, which isn't dishonest. To keep the front element of your lens clean and safe, any of the above will suffice, but if you're looking to protect your lens *and* improve the image quality of your stills and video, you're going to want to purchase a UV or Skylight filter.

UV filters, also referred to as Haze filters, are designed to cut through the effects of atmospheric haze, moisture and other forms of airborne pollutants, each of which contributes to image degradation. UV/Haze filters are available in varying strengths. If you plan on photographing near large bodies of open water, at higher altitudes, in snow or other conditions that magnify the intensity of ambient ultra-violet light, you should definitely consider a stronger level of UV filtration (UV-410, UV-415, UV-420, UV-Haze 2A, UV-Haze 2B, UV-Haze 2C and UV-Haze 2E). Depending on the strength of the UV coatings, UV filters appear clear, or in the case of heavier UV coatings, have a warm, amber-like appearance and require anywhere from zero to about a half stop of exposure compensation.

An alternative to UV/Haze filters are Skylight filters, which are available in a choice of two strengths—Skylight 1A and Skylight 1B. Unlike UV/Haze filters, which have a warm amber appearance, Skylight filters have a magenta tint that is preferable when photographing skin tones or using color slide film, which depending on the film stock often has a blue bias that is typically counterbalanced by the magenta tint of Skylight filters.

Regardless of their strength, skylight filters do not have any effect on the camera exposure, are equal to UV filters in terms of cutting through atmospheric haze and protect your lens against dust, moisture and fingerprints that can all be damaging to lens coatings if not removed in a timely manner.

If you photograph landscapes—or any outdoor scenic for that matter—you should certainly have a **Polarizing filter** handy at all times. Polarizing filters are best known for making clouds seemingly pop out from darkened blue skies, saturating colors and eliminating glare and reflections from the surfaces of water, glass and other polished surfaces.

Polarizing filters are mounted in a secondary ring that you manually rotate while viewing your subject through the viewfinder until you dial in the desired level of Polarization. The downside of Polarizing filters is that you lose about three stops of light in the process of optimizing the image, but the results cannot be mimicked using Photoshop plug-ins or other forms of post-capture voodoo.

Polarizing filters are also available combined with additional filtration such as warming filtration (81A, 81C, 81EF, 85, 85B), Enhancing and Intensifying, Skylight, UV/Haze and a measure of diffusion.

Polarizing filters are available in two formats: linear and circular. Though they look and perform identically, circular Polarizing filters are designed specifically for use with autofocus lenses while linear are best used with manual-focus lenses. Circular Polarizers, on the other hand, can be used with AF or MF optics with equal results.

Neutral density (ND) filters are essentially gray-toned filters designed to absorb calibrated degrees of light as it passes through the lens. Most commonly broken down in 1/3, 2/3 and full-stop increments, ND filters are more recently also available as variable-density filters that you can infinitely adjust by rotating the filter on its mount as you would a Polarizing filter.

There are many applications for ND filters. Chief among them is their ability to allow you to shoot at wider f-stops under bright lighting conditions. ND filters are used extensively by filmmakers and videographers as tools that allow them better exposure control due to the limited shutter-speed options afforded by the cinema and video process. ND filters also make it possible to blur the movement of pedestrian traffic and flowing water under bright lighting conditions by allowing you to drop your shutter speeds while maintaining full control of how much or how little depth of field you desire, based on the amount of ND filtration you place in front of the lens.

There is a Graduated ND filter also. Now one question here arises is that what's the difference between Neutral Density and Graduated Neutral Density Filters?

Neutral density filters are even, edge to edge, in their degree of density while graduated neutral density filters are typically clear on one end and slowly build up density toward the opposite side of the filter. Graduated ND filters are most commonly used to even out scenes containing extreme exposure variations on opposite sides of the frame.

Without graduated neutral density filter (L); with graduated neutral density filter (R)

Examples of these types of scenarios include landscapes in which the top of a mountain is bathed in sunlight, while the valley below lies in shade; and multi-story atriums where the primary source of illumination is an overhead skylight from which the light gradually falls off as it approaches the lower levels. Graduated filters can also be used in evenly lit areas to darken the sky or foreground for stylistic reasons.

In addition to neutral graduated filters, colored grad filters are also available, and are useful for adding a touch of subliminal color into a scene while darkening the foreground or background.

Should I consider warming and cooling filters?

While warming (adding yellow to the scene) and cooling (adding blue to the scene) can be applied to an image file post capture in Photoshop or other image-editing software, there are still those—including film shooters, who prefer to filter the lens at the time the exposure is made.

Most photographers warm or cool their images for aesthetic or mood reasons. A bit of warming is often desired for portraits, or when photographing at midday during the summer months when the sun's light can be bluer and harsh. Warming can also be effective when taking pictures on overcast or rainy days.

Conversely, <u>cooling filters</u> can be used to correct color in images in which the color temperature is too warm to suit your intentions. Warming filters include all <u>81 and 85-series filters</u>, and cooling filters include all <u>80 and 82-series filters</u>.

When using cooling, warming and other color filters with digital cameras, it's important to set the White Balance to a setting close to the ambient color temperature, i.e. Daylight, Overcast, Tungsten, Fluorescent, etc., and avoid Auto WB, which will intuitively try to correct, according to its own parameters, the mood and tone you're trying to establish. Auto WB may not render results that are in agreement with your personal vision.

<u>**Color-correction filters**</u>, also called <u>cc filters</u>, consist of cyan, magenta, yellow, red, green and blue filters. Each of these is available in 10% increments and is used for modifying or correcting the color balance of mismatched or irregular light sources. The need for cc filters is not as great in these digital days as it was in the time of film. Nevertheless, they are still used by many photographers who would rather correct their images at the time of capture.

As with warming, cooling and other color filters, it's advisable to avoid the Auto WB setting on your digital camera when using cc filters and instead choose daylight, overcast, tungsten, fluorescent or whatever setting is closest to the ambient lighting conditions under which you're working.

Slim filters : This type of filters have narrow profiles and sometimes lack threads on the forward side of the filter ring. Slim filters, which are available in almost every filter size, are designed for use with lenses featuring angles of view wider than about 74°, or the equivalent of a 28mm lens. By utilizing a thinner retaining ring, the filter is less likely to vignette the corners of the frame. Depending on the make and model, many kit zooms require thin or slim-mount filters.

TYPES OF CINEMATIC SHOTS

PAN SHOT, Used to:
-Include space greater than can be viewed through a fixed frame
-Follow action as it moves
-Connect two or more points of interest graphically
-Connect of imply a logical connection between two or more subjects

CRANE SHOT

-Inherently majestic and holds our interest regardless of the subject because of the sheer physical pleasure of the move

-Permits us to feel the dimensions of the world by penetrating space, further endorsing its reality through the illusion of depth

-Eats up time on the set

-Careful planning and preparation is vital

TRACKING SHOT

-Used to follow a subject or explore space

-A dolly moves towards subjects face can be used to emphasize a character's moment of realization. A dolly always tends to isolate the subject as well

TRIPOD SHOTS

-Usually is used only in stable and relatively predictable shooting situations

-Makes very controlled transitions from subject to subject possible

-Makes very controlled image transitions possible

-Makes stable close-ups possible at the telephoto end of the zoom lens

-Conveys the cool, assured view

HANDHELD SHOTS

-Can react to events, much as we do in life

-Implies a spontaneous event driven quest

-Conveys a subjective, even vulnerable point of view.

ANALYSIS OF ANY GIVEN SHOT – TWELVE ELEMENTS

1) SHOT AND CAMERA PROXEMICS

-What type of shot is it? How far away from the action is the camera?

2) ANGLE

-Are we looking up or down on the subject, or is the camera neutral?

3) LENS or FILTER
-How do these distort or comment on the photographed materials?

4) LIGHTING STYLE
-High or low key lighting? High contrast? Some combination of these?

5) DOMINANT
-Where is our eye attracted first?

6) SUBSIDIARIES
-Where does our eye travel after taking in the dominant?

7) COMPOSITION
-How is the two-dimensional space segmented and organized? What is the underlying design?

8) FORM
-Open or closed? Does the image suggest a window that arbitrarily isolates a fragment of the scene? How are the visual elements carefully arranged and held in balance?

9) FRAMING
-Tight or loose? Do the characters have room to move around in, or can they move freely?

10) DEPTH
-On how many planes is the image composed? What do we see in the background?

11) STAGING PROBLEMS
-Which way do the characters look from the camera?

12) CHARACTER PROXEMICS
-How much space is there between the characters?

MOVEMENT IS NOT SIMPLY A MATTER OF WHAT HAPPENS, BUT HOW THINGS HAPPEN.

The OBSERVER has to be the CAMERA and it needs to know where it's going.
THE VALUE OF A SHOT ALWAYS DEPENDS ON A NARRATIVE.

THE PRINCIPLES OF PERSPECTIVE

-Finding the right points of the sequence and getting to tell the best narrative story.

AESTHETIC DISTANCE – Phrase used to describe the degree to which a work or art manipulates the viewer.

FIRST PERSON POINT OF VIEW – Sees events through the eyes of the character.

THIRD PERSON POINT OF VIEW – Presents action as seen by an ideal observer.

OMNISCIENT POINT OF VIEW – Having to know what the character is thinking. Requires a type of narration, voice-over or graphics.

SOME MORE IMPORTANT CINEMATOGRAPHY TERMS

Aspect ratio and framing

The aspect ratio of an image is the ratio of its width to its height. This can be expressed either as a ratio of 2 integers, such as 4:3, or in a decimal format, such as 1.33:1 or simply 1.33.

Different ratios provide different aesthetic effects. Standards for aspect ratio have varied significantly over time.

During the silent era, aspect ratios varied widely, from square 1:1, all the way up to the extreme widescreen 4:1 Polyvision. However, from the 1910s, silent motion pictures generally settled on the ratio of 4:3 (1.33). The introduction of sound-on-film briefly narrowed the aspect ratio, to allow room for a sound stripe. In 1932, a new standard was introduced, the Academy ratio of 1.37, by means of thickening the frame line.

For years, mainstream cinematographers were limited to using the Academy ratio, but in the 1950s, thanks to the popularity of Cinerama, widescreen ratios were introduced in an effort to pull audiences back into the theater and away from their home television sets. These new widescreen formats provided cinematographers a wider frame within which to compose their images.

Many different proprietary photographic systems were invented and used in the 1950s to create widescreen movies, but one dominated film: the anamorphic process, which optically squeezes the image to photograph twice the horizontal area to the same size vertical as standard "spherical" lenses. The first commonly used anamorphic format was Cinemascope, which used a 2.35 aspect ratio, although it was originally 2.55. Cinemascope was used from 1953 to 1967, but due to technical flaws in the design and its ownership by Fox, several third-party companies, led by Panavision's technical improvements in the 1950s, dominated the anamorphic cine lens market. Changes to SMPTE projection standards altered the projected ratio from 2.35 to 2.39 in 1970, although this did not change anything regarding the photographic anamorphic standards; all changes in respect to the aspect ratio of anamorphic 35 mm photography are specific to camera or projector gate sizes, not the optical system. After the "widescreen wars" of the 1950s, the motion-picture industry settled into 1.85 as a standard for theatrical projection in the United States and the United Kingdom. This is a cropped version of 1.37. Europe and Asia opted for 1.66 at first, although 1.85 has largely permeated these markets in recent decades. Certain "epic" or adventure movies utilized the anamorphic 2.39 (often incorrectly denoted '2.40').

In the 1990s, with the advent of high-definition video, television engineers created the 1.78 (16:9) ratio as a mathematical compromise between the theatrical standard of 1.85 and television's 1.33, as it was not practical to produce a traditional CRT television tube with a width of 1.85. Until that change, nothing had ever been originated in 1.78. Today, this is a standard for high-definition video and for widescreen television.

LIGHTING

Light is necessary to create an image exposure on a frame of film or on a digital target. The art of lighting for cinematography goes far beyond basic exposure, however, into the essence of visual storytelling. Lighting contributes considerably to the emotional response an audience has watching a motion picture. The increased usage of filters can greatly impact the final image and affect the lighting.

There is a universally followed four point light setup used in film shooting :

Key light, Fill light, Back light and Background light.

The key light, as the name suggests, shines directly upon the subject and serves as its principal illuminator; more than anything else, the strength, color and angle of the key determines the shot's overall lighting design.

In indoor shots, the key is commonly a specialized lamp, or a camera's flash. In outdoor daytime shots, the Sun often serves as the key light. In this case, of course, the photographer cannot set the light in the exact position they want, so instead arranges the shot to best capture the sunlight, perhaps after waiting for the sun to position itself just right.

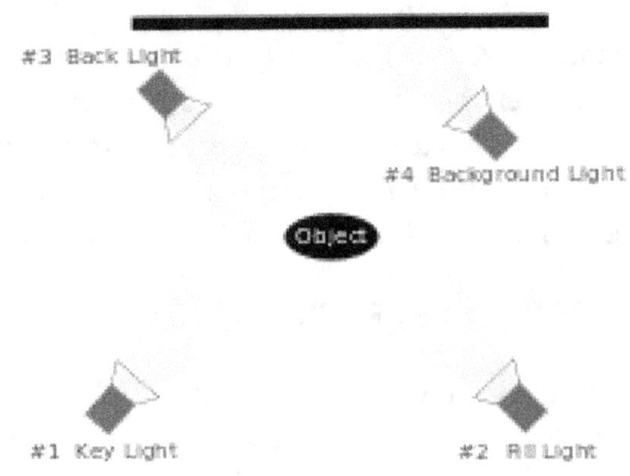

The fill light also shines on the subject, but from a side angle relative to the key and is often placed at a lower position than the key (about at the level of the subject's face). It balances the key by illuminating shaded surfaces, and lessening or eliminating chiaroscuro effects, such as the shadow cast by a person's nose upon the rest of the face. It is usually softer and less bright than the key light (up to half), and more to a flood. Not using a fill at all can result in stark contrasts (due to shadows) across the subject's surface, depending upon the key light's harshness. Sometimes, as in low-key lighting, this is a deliberate effect, but shots intended to look more natural and less stylistic require a fill.

In some situations a photographer can use a reflector (such as a piece of white cardstock mounted off-camera, or even a white-painted wall) as a fill light instead of an actual lamp. Reflecting and redirecting the key light's rays back upon the subject from a different angle can cause a softer, subtler effect than using another lamp.

The <u>backlight</u> (a.k.a. the rim, hair, or shoulder light) shines on the subject from behind, often (but not necessarily) to one side or the other. It gives the subject a rim of light, serving to separate the subject from the background and highlighting contours.

Back light or rim light is different from a kick in that a kick (or kicker) contributes to a portion of the shading on the visible surface of the subject, while a rim light only creates a thin outline around the subject without necessarily hitting the front (visible) surface of the subject at all.

The addition of a fourth light, the <u>background light</u>, makes for a four-point lighting setup.

The background light is placed behind the subject(s), on a high grid, or low to the ground. Unlike the other three lights, which illuminate foreground elements like actors and props, it illuminates background elements, such as walls or outdoor scenery. This technique can be used to eliminate shadows cast by foreground elements onto the background, or to draw more attention to the background. It also helps to off-set the single eye nature of the camera, this means that it helps the camera give depth to the subject.

CINEMATOGRAPHY FOR SCREENWRITERS

Screenwriting students are often told to think visually. This is good advice. But it might be even more correct to say, "Think cinema." Modern practice calls for specific camera angles and shots to be left largely up to the director. Directors (and therefore producers) do not want scripts filled with camera shots specified. Only if it is important to understanding the action should a camera shot be put in a script.

However, this does not mean that a screenwriter should not understand something about cinematography. Screenplays are often described as blueprints for films. Imagine an architect trying to draw a blueprint for a building without knowing anything about the materials it was to be constructed from. To effectively design a script, a screenwriter should know something about cinematography and editing. Only then can he write knowledgeably for the medium.

A film is composed of many shots. For the cinematographer and editor, the job is to pick the right shots which will, at any given moment, best convey the story clearly to the audience as well as heightening the impact of the action and characters. In choosing any particular shot, there are two factors to consider: the type of shot in terms of the area to be shown and the angle or viewpoint of the shot. In a script, the screenwriter will very occasionally have to specify both of these to make clear his vision. But he should do this only when absolutely necessary for the simple reason that directors tend to ignore camera cues in a script and think the writer is trying to do their job for them. However, as mentioned previously, the writer can write his scene descriptions in such a way as to suggest the cinematographic treatment of his action. And doing this will help the reader better visualize the film.

So thinking visually is only part of a screenwriter's skill. He must also be able to think cinema- graphically. This condenses action down to a shot by shot telling of the story. When you visualize the action, consider how the camera can show this action. And then write your scene descriptions so they capture the flavor of this.

Learn to think cinema- graphically in visualizing your scenes. Next we move to editing and continuity part of the film language element.

Continuity

In the early days of motion pictures, shooting scripts were sometimes called continuity scripts. This is because they consisted of the plan for shooting a script so that continuity was maintained for the audience.

Continuity is the way a film is shot and cut together so that, for the audience, it will have the appearance of a smooth, logical flow of action. As soon as the continuity is not maintained, this will distract an audience and lose their attention. A film with good continuity is designed to attract and keep the audience's attention. For the director, the cinematographer and the editor, action must be planned in a series of shots which make up a sequence. These shots must cut together so that edits are not jerky or jarring to the audience.

While this is not a major concern of the screenwriter, it is nevertheless to your advantage to understand at least a few of the rudimentary rules of continuity:

1) The time frame of a movie must be preserved for the audience. Flashbacks (or the occasional flash forward) must be filmed in such a way that the audience knows there has been a shift of movie time. They must immediately realize that they are not in the present movie time, but in some other time. Flashbacks should generally be used sparingly, if at all, because they disrupt the film's time.

2) The space continuity of the film must also be preserved. This includes establishing and then maintaining screen direction. A car seen traveling left to right on the screen can not in the next shot be traveling right to left. The audience would interpret this as the car having turned around and headed back in the opposite direction.
If one had two groups headed towards each other, one might have one traveling from left to right and the other traveling from right to left. The audience would interpret this as the two groups heading towards each

other.
Similarly, someone facing toward the left cannot, in the next shot, be facing toward the right if they are supposed to be in the same position. This will jar the audience and cause a slight bit of confusion.

3) Cuts must be matched in terms of actor positions, looks and movement so that the audience does not notice these cuts. A minor mismatch may go unnoticed if the camera has shifted angle as well as position. Editors will often try to cut on action rather than static shots, as the motion will sometimes help to mask a slight mismatch.

Editors will also use a technique known as the cut-away. In this, an editor cuts to something which was not a portion of a previous shot. Then cutting back to the character again does not have to match the previous shot on the character and the audience will not notice the jump.

Cutting from a long shot to a close-up also allows a certain amount of "cheating."

The size of the image and the angle of the camera have a great deal to do with acceptable continuity. A cut between one image to a very similar shot of the same image with only a slight change in size will be noticed by the audience. There is insufficient contrast between succeeding images to allow for a smooth transition. The same principle applies to a change of angle between two shots cut together. Cutting from a medium shot to a close-up usually requires a change of camera angle to cut smoothly. Otherwise the image will seem to jump to the audience.

In a more general sense, a script has to maintain continuity by following a logical sequence. When you specify cross-cutting between two different scenes, this must be done to increase the impact, tension and contrast. The action in the two scenes obviously must relate in some way. Otherwise, the cross-cutting will just be distracting. If you think in sequences, you will tend to write a script where continuity is preserved and which, therefore, allows the audience to become involved with the story.

Editing

The various shots are just so many odd pieces of film until they are skillfully assembled to tell a coherent story. Both a diamond and a film are enhanced by what is removed, he said. What remains tells the story.

A screenwriter should have at least a general understanding of the principles of editing. It is editing which helps to create the pace and texture of a film.

The fundamental principles of editing were developed during the early days of silent films. The introduction of sound brought some minor changes. The determination of pace, which in the silent days depended entirely on the rate of cutting, was augmented by the volume and urgency of the sound-track.

In fact, the main change that the advent of sound brought was to increase the realism of films. In editing, this change saw certain editing techniques fall out of general use--those styles which tend to distract from the realism, such as masking of part of the image so that the viewer only saw a character surrounded by a distinctive masked border.

The use of close, medium and long shots for different emphasis has not changed. However, with stars having become a commodity to increase box-office, sometimes too many close-ups are used to capitalize upon the presence of the star at the expense of the film's pace and movement. A close-up has a specific purpose and a specific time to be used.

There has been little change in the role that timing or tempo of cuts plays in helping to produce dramatic tension. The faster the cutting, the more urgent the pace will seem to the audience. Cross-cutting increases tension by alternate cutting between two events which have a direct bearing on each other. Events can also be cross-cut to achieve contrast or comparison. A rapid cross-cut sequence is often saved to coincide with the climax, to heighten the tension and suspense at this point. In film, there is the possibility of lengthening or shortening the duration of an event. This makes possible the cutting down of unnecessary intervals. This is what is meant by screen time being different from real time.

As well, film editing enables the director and editor to present a series of consecutive events in such a way that each new development is revealed at the dramatically appropriate moment. The pace of a scene is determined both by its content and by the speed with which various shots are cut. By increasing the speed of cutting within a sequence, the impression of fast, exciting action can be created. But to really work well, the pace of cutting has to match the content and the amount of information being conveyed in each shot. A writer who understands a little about general editing principles will have more control over the pacing of his script. For instance, in a fast and exciting action scene, he should write it so the cutting can be rapid. Lengthy pieces of dialogue would not fit here.

Transitions

Transitions are devices used to bridge time or space in a film. The simplest transition is simply a title on the screen indicating a different time or place. There are also optical effects which can help to bridge a change in time or place.

A FADE-IN begins a story and a FADE-OUT ends it. A fade-out and then a fade-in can be used to end one sequence and start a new.

A DISSOLVE, fading-out one scene while another is fading-in at the same time, can also cover time lapses, change of locale or be used to soften an abrupt scene change that would otherwise jar the audience.

MATCHED DISSOLVES are those where the two connected scenes are similar in form, motion or contentand can further enhance the smoothness of the transition.

Sound can also be used to effect a smoother transition. Narration or dialogue can cover a switch in location or can explain a time change. For instance, a line of dialogue may say, "Let's go." Then the cut is to the going.

SOUND

Arguably the most subtly influential aspect of film

There are three components of sound in film: dialogue, sound effects, and music Music is often the most evident and recognisable component of sound. Dialogue and sound effects, while more subdued in effect than music, are essential in bringing us into the world of the film and suspending our belief.

Three types of sound are classified as Diegetic, Non-diegetic and Trans-diegetic.

What Is Diegetic Sound?

Diegetic sound is any sound that emanates from the storyworld of the film. The term comes from the word diegesis, which is the evolution of a Greek term that means narration or narrative.

The source of diegetic sound doesn't necessarily need to be seen on screen, as long as the audience understands that it is coming from something within the film.

How Is Diegetic Sound Made?

Just because a diegetic sound emanates from the world of story, doesn't necessarily mean that it was recorded that day on set. Many diegetic sounds are actually recorded in a studio by sound engineers, making the sounds clearer. For example:

- The director forgot to shoot a line of dialogue on set, so the actor will re-record that line in the studio in post-production. This is called ADR.
- A party scene doesn't sound exciting enough, so the sound editor will punch up the sound of laughter, music, or ambient noise to create a livelier party atmosphere.

Three examples of Diegetic Sound

1. **Character dialogue** is the clearest example of diegetic sound.
2. **Object sounds** make a film more realistic. For example, if a character walks in the snow, the audience should hear the crunching of their footsteps. If a character is standing on a busy street, we hear the natural ambiance of the city.
3. **Music emanating from within in the film** helps the audience become absorbed in a scene. For example, music playing loudly in someone's headphones, or the pounding dance music at a bar are also diegetic sound. This kind of diegetic sound is also called "diegetic music" or "source music."

What Is Non-Diegetic Sound?

Non-diegetic sound, also called commentary or nonliteral sound, is any sound that does not originate from within the film's world. The film's characters are not able to hear non-diegetic sound. All non-diegetic sound is added by sound editors in post-production.

Three examples of Non-Diegetic Sound

1. **The film's musical score** is used to set the film's tone, manipulate emotions, add drama, express ambiguity, or provide an element of surprise.
2. **Sound effects** are added for dramatic effect. For example, a record scratch sound added for comic relief is not heard by the characters in the film.
3. **Narration or voice over** is used to help explain or reinforce the plot.

What Is Trans-Diegetic Sound?

When diegetic and non-diegetic sound are combined, it's called trans-diegetic. Trans-diegetic sound refers to any sound that moves in between non-diegetic and diegetic, or vice versa. Trans-diegetic sound helps **bridge or link** two things, like transitions between scenes.

Two examples of Trans-Diegetic Sound and When a Filmmaker Should Use It

1. A character hums a tune (diegetic sound) and that humming sound turns into an orchestral version of the same tune (non-diegetic sound), which carries over into the next scene.
2. Music plays over the opening credits of a film (non-diegetic sound), but once the title sequence ends, that same music becomes a song heard on someone's radio in the opening scene (diegetic sound). This example links the credit sequence with the opening scene to ease the audience into the movie-going experience.

Film Direction

Even though they may not appear in front of the camera, the director is one of the most important people on a film set. They do more than shout "action" and "cut" behind the scenes—they're the person who determines the creative vision and makes all of the film's biggest decisions. A director is a person who determines the creative vision of a feature film, television show, play, short film, or other production. They have complete artistic control of a project. In addition to having a strong grasp of technical knowledge taught in directing classes, they must also have a personal or emotional connection to the material.

What Does a Director Do During Pre-production?

- **Assemble a team.** The first people you'll need are a line producer, production designer, location manager, cinematographer, and assistant director.
- **Create your vision for the film and communicate it to your crew.** Establish a visual language for your film by creating a lookbook. Fill it with reference images to help you articulate your ideal color palette, locations, and framing. It helps to reference other films that inspire you.
- **Discuss your vision with each key crew member individually.** Your vision affects every department differently. For example, if you say, "I want it to feel like the character is isolated," that affects lens choice, lighting, and music. Learn to speak the language of every department so you can successfully communicate what you need from them.

- **Make casting choices**. You can change many of your decisions along the way, but casting is the least flexible in terms of making last-minute changes. Before you cast an actor, it's important that they understand the story you're telling. They should be someone you trust to prepare the role to the best of their ability and who is willing to be flexible and collaborate with you.

What Does a Director Do During Production?

- **Guide the actors through scenes**. It's your job to help inform and shape their performances, so give the actors positive but specific (and short) praise and/or notes after every take. Make sure you're on the same page about who the characters are and what they want in each scene.
- **Ensure every department is doing its job**. You're the person who is most familiar with every part of the production. You must make sure every department is doing its job and working together to bring the film to life.
- **Communicate with everyone as much as possible**. Directing is a collaborative process. Having open communication with every team is vital to making the best film possible so everyone feels comfortable speaking up and knows exactly what they need to be doing.
- **Keep your artistic vision alive**. Continue to check in with every department, from the producers to the actors to the crew, about what you need from them in order to translate your creative vision to the screen.

What Does a Director Do During Post-production?

- **Give notes to the editor**. Review the editor's cuts, break down the footage, and find the shots, angles, and takes that add the most meaning.
- **Check in with post-production teams**. Work with the sound design team, the music supervisor, and the visual effects team to ensure every postproduction decision is in line with your overall vision.
- **Give final signoff**. You have complete creative control, and it's up to you to determine when a project is finished.

Next we move on to seven steps a director should follow :

STEP 1: The Study of Human Behavior

What do I mean by the study of human behavior?

The study of human behavior is about:

a. What makes us tick?
b. Why do we do things?

Once you know the answers to these questions, you will have a better idea of how the characters in your script should interact with each other, as well as having the proper "psychological tools" to direct actors on the set.

The good thing about human behavior is that it is observable, and as storytellers, we must first observe the way people react to different situations and circumstances in order to understand How and Why their behavior changes.

As a film director, you must be a "witness" to human behavior. You need to get into the habit of observing people going about their daily lives, so you can find out what motivates them to take action.

Once you know what motivates a person to achieve their daily needs, you will have the knowledge to better understand the story you are telling, and you will feel more confident helping your actors achieve believable performances.

STEP 2: Story

There are many facets of a Director's prep on any film or TV show, but the first, and most important part of your job, is to understand every detail about the story: where it takes place; who the characters are; and what happens to them.

When you first read a script, here are just some of the many questions you will need to answer to help identify and solve potential script problems:

a. What is the story about?

b. Does the story make sense?

c. What problem is to be resolved?

d. What event hooks the audience?

e. What is the plot? (the action)

f. What is the subplot? (the theme)

Understanding the story requires a lot of work on your part because you then need to take dig deeper into the story and it's structure by analyzing each individual scene in the script to find out what it is about, what works and what doesn't by asking questions like:

a. What is the intention of the scene?

b. What are the story points?

c. Where are the scene beats?

d. Where is the climax?

e. What is the resolution?

f. What are the important lines of dialogue?

Your script breakdown will be a never-ending process. Each time you read the script, you will find something else you didn't know about the story or the characters.

And the script will also constantly evolve. It will change because of your creative notes, writer changes, actor changes, producer changes, studio changes and location availability.

But as long as you know what the story is about, and where the story is going, you will be able to adjust to all the changes.

STEP 3: Performance

I believe that almost everything you need to know about directing actors is explained in these three words:

MOTIVE DETERMINES BEHAVIOUR

When we break these words down, we see that:

MOTIVE (our inner world)
DETERMINES (controls)
BEHAVIOUR (our outer world)

And if we break them down even further, we see that:

What our needs are (MOTIVE)
Will decide (DETERMINES)
What actions we will take (BEHAVIOUR)

One of the main responsibilities of a Director is to help actors achieve a realistic performance, and a good director does this by "listening for the truth" and by always asking:

a. Do I believe them?

b. Do the words make sense?

c. Are the characters believable?

And the key to getting a realistic performance from an actor, is by first understanding a character's objectives.

a. There should be one main objective per character per scene: What do they want in the scene?

b. Objectives should be clear, concise and stated in one simple sentence: "To discover where the gun is hidden."

How to choose objectives:

a. Ask yourself "What does the character want in this situation?"

b. A character's objective should create obstacles for the character.

c. Look at what the character does (his behaviour) rather than what he says.

d. Look at what happens in the scene, and how it ends.

e. Look at what people want out of life: what are the things we will sacrifice everything for?

On the set, actors want to work with directors who understand their vulnerability, so it's incredibly important to create a good relationship with every actor on your film.

And what do actors want more than anything from this relationship with the director? TRUST!

If actors feel they cannot trust the director to know a good performance from a bad performance, they will begin to monitor their own performances and begin to direct themselves: they will become "Director Proof!"

Remember, to find the character they are playing, actors must surrender completely to feelings and impulses, and a good director understands an actor's vulnerability and creates a safe place for them to perform.

STEP 4: The Principles of Montage

One of the key elements of being a good director, is to understand the "principles of montage" – the juxtaposition of images to tell a story.

In 1918, a Russian filmmaker called Lev Kuleshov conducted an experiment where he shot and edited a short film in which the face of a famous Russian matinee idol was intercut with three other shots: a plate of soup; a girl playing ball; an old woman in a coffin.

And Kuleshov made sure that the shot of the actor was identical (and expressionless) every time he cut back to him.

The film was then shown to audiences who totally believed that the expression on the actor's face was different each time he appeared – depending on whether he was "looking at" the plate of soup, the little girl, or the old woman's coffin; showing an expression of hunger, happiness or grief respectively.

So what does this experiment tell us?

By carefully using the juxtaposition of images, filmmakers were able to produce certain emotions from the audience by manipulating an actor's performance.

As a film director, understanding the principles of montage will help you to: create a more visual script; to decide your camera placement; to block your scenes; and to get layered performances from actors.

STEP 5: The Psychology of the Camera

What I mean by the Psychology of the Camera are the visual meanings of shots and angles. In other words, where you put the camera can either enhance or detract the audience's understanding of what the scene is really about, and what the characters are feeling. For example:

There are three angles of view for the camera:

a. Objective: The audience point of view. (The camera is placed outside the action.)

b. Subjective: The camera acts as the viewer's eyes. (The camera is placed inside the action.)

c. Point of View: What the character is seeing. (The camera is the action.)

Audiences will assume that every shot or word of dialogue in a film is there to further the central idea, therefore, each shot you use should contribute to the story or the idea you are trying to convey.

Since viewer emotion is the ultimate goal of each scene, where you place the camera involves knowing what emotion you want the audience to experience, at any given moment in the scene.

STEP 6: Basic Blocking & Staging Techniques

Very simply, blocking is the relationship of the actors to the camera. Blocking is not about getting the dialogue correct or discussing an actor's motivation – unless it directly involves the movement of an actor.

I suggest you start thinking of blocking as the choreography of a dance or ballet: all the elements on the set (actors, extras, vehicles, crew, equipment) should move in perfect harmony with each other.

Before you start to figure out your blocking plan, you must know these five things:

a. When, and where, were the characters last seen?

b. What is the last shot of the previous scene?

c. What is the first shot of the scene you are working on?

d. What is the last shot of the scene you are working on?

e. What is the first shot of the next scene?

Your blocking plan will also be determined by:

a. Whose POV is being expressed at the time? (Is it the writer's, the character or the director?)

b. What distance are you from the subject? (What is the size of shot: close or far?)

c. What is your relationship to the subject? (What is the angle of view – your choice of lenses?)

When you first start directing, blocking a scene can be one of the hardest parts of your job. But like anything else in life, blocking takes practice, and the more times you do it, the more comfortable you will become.

STEP 7: Technical

By technical, I mean everything else it takes to make a movie!
(Locations, Cinematography, Editing, Sound, Costumes, Stunts...)

Yes, I know I'm putting the majority of the filmmaking process into one category, but without understanding the first 6 steps of this formula, you are setting yourself up for "filmmaker mediocrity" – which is writing unimaginative scripts with unbelievable characters that create boring and dull films.

We can now summarize the above mentioned things till now as Micro and Macro elements in film

Micro elements consist of four things:
A. Cinematography : It is the camera angles and movements. Different angles add a different effect to the scene. For example, a low angle makes the character on screen look powerful and a high angle makes the character look weak. Also a 360 degree shot makes the character look confused. The different camera

angles are Low angles, High angles, Long shot, Wide shot, Close up, Extreme close up, Mid shot, Point of view and Over the shoulder. The different camera movements are Panning, Tilting, 360 degree, Steadicam, Tracking shot and Crane shot. Low Angle= Power Wide shot= to see the surroundings High angle= submissive Mid shot= see character arm movements Long shot= centre of attention (power)

Point of view= allows audience to experience the movie through character's eyes Over the shoulder= see chemistry between both characters in one shot Extreme close up= conceals identity and surroundings of characters Close up= see character's facial expressions

Panning shot= shows setting Tracking shot Steadicam shot= puts audience in the movie. Titling shot= power Crane shot 360 degree shot= Confusion.

B. Mise en scene: It is a term for what is in the shot. This includes the lighting, colours used, props and their placement, setting/location, makeup and costumes. All these factors make up the scene and enhances the effect the producer and director is trying to show the audience. An example is: The red costume connotes danger and blood which alerts the audience. The low lighting used makes the scene look more eerie causing the audience to panic. The use of the crosses is an irony as in this scene there is an evil spirit, something that is not associated with Christianity. The pale makeup makes her seem ghastly to create distress in the audience. The house with broken furniture tells the audience that they are about to see something destructive and bad.

C. Sound: There are different sounds that are included in film. Diegetic sounds are sounds that are made in the in the scene and the source it is coming from is visible to the audience for example, dialogue, music by characters and sounds made by objects in the scene e.g. footsteps. Non- diegetic sounds are sounds that come from a source not visible on the screen for example, background music and narrator commentary. Sound can be both off-screen and on-screen for example if the source of the sound is not shown on screen but is made in the studio for example someone shouting from the distance then it is an off- screen sound as it is not in the frame. An on-screen sound is when the source is seen in the frame for example the dialogue by a character talking to another character.

D. Editing There are different styles of editing. Editing links two shots together and there are times when there is movement from one shot to another, this is called a transition. There are many transitions, straight cut which is when it jumps from one shot to another shot with not effects, a fade which is when the screen goes black or white to show time passing, a dissolve to show the passing of time of that the scene showing is happening at the same time as the previous scene, wipe shots to show a jump in time and graphic shots which is when an object from the first shot turns into an object in the second shot for example in Psycho, the eye turns to a drain to show a possible link. There are four different styles of continuity editing. This includes the eye-line match which occurs when you see a shot of the character in the centre of the frame looking at an object which u can see on the corner of the frame then you see a shot of the object in the centre and the person looking at it from the corner of the frame. There is a Match-on-action shot which is when we see a character doing something that is continue over to another shot which is done by taking various shots of the exact same movement but putting the camera in different places. Furthermore, there is the 180 degree rule which is an imaginary line which goes between two characters on screen and the camera, when broken it will look flipped so one character will start off on one side then change positions then back again which does not look good to the audience. Finally, the shot reverse shot is when you see a shot of a character looking at an object which is off screen, then the camera cuts to a shot of the object.

Macro Elements There are four elements to Macro elements:
Narrative : It is the structure of the film for example at the beginning of the film, the characters are sometimes introduced by the narrator or the audience gets to know their name through a conversation between characters. There will be an equilibrium where everything is how it should be, following with a disruption usually caused by a villain, leading to a resolution which closes the film with a new equilibrium. This kind of narrative is a narrative that follows the Todorov's Theory. You could also say that this is similar to the Classic Hollywood narrative as the new equilibrium is a closure which is how most Hollywood film go. However, there are subplots involved in the classic Hollywood narrative for example another disruption may be introduced during the film. A Three act structure is similar to both narratives as this narrative involves 3 parts to a film which is the set up is 25% of the film, the confrontation is 50% and the final is 25%. This narrative could also be called a typical Hollywood structure. Another Narrative is the Roland Barthes theory which is when the text has many meanings and they are complex for example you could have an open text which is when the problem is not resolved at the end or you could have a closed text which is when the disruption is resolved. You could also have a polysemic text which is when the ending has different meaning for example they could be dead in real life but lives in an alternative universe. Most films have a binary opposite narrative which is when there is a villain vs a hero or a dominant character vs subordinate character .

Genre: There are different genres of films for example Horror which contains frightening scenes and ghost. Thrillers which has a villain and hero and thrills the audience. Adventure which has characters that go on adventures and encounter a few problems on their quest. Comedy which contains humor and sometimes love between two characters (romcom). Romance which has a storyline between two characters falling in love. Action which contain a lot of fast paced action scenes and hero vs villain scenes. Animation mostly watched by kids. Sci-fi which are usually set in space or in another time (mainly in the future). There are many more film genres such as drama, war, fiction, etc.

Representation : There are different types of representation seen in films for example male actors move the plot forward, they seem more superior and they do most of the action and hard work whereas the females are used as sexual item and they do most of the light work for example chores. There is also a representation of class seen in many films for example people in the upper class live a good live, has valuables and are very social. This might apply to some middle class characters while the rest along with the lower class have a very simple life, they do not own luxury items and they are not seen with other groups of people. The women look scared and vulnerable while the man looks on in confidence.

Audience : The audience is a key factor to any film. Film producers try to aim at certain audiences whether it's male or female and through their age too for example, Marvel is known for its many superhero films. They all appeal to the male audience as they are known to like these types of films whereas females would rather sit a watch a romcom or an action. Marvel films usually appeal to young adults, teens, children and some adults. Film producers also try to make films that the audience knows what to expect from it for example, horror films are known for their stupid characters, same narrative and cliches such as jump scares. Sometimes producers do the opposite to make films more interesting.

ACTING & IMPROVISATION

The basic definition of acting recognized worldwide is that it is to react according to a given situation. It is an activity in which a story is told by means of its enactment by an actor or actress who adopts a character—in theatre, television, film, radio, or any other medium that makes use of the mimeticmode.

Acting involves a broad range of skills, including a well-developed imagination, emotional facility, physical expressivity, vocal projection, clarity of speech, and the ability to interpret drama. Acting also demands an ability to employ dialects, accents, improvisation, observation and emulation, mime, and stage combat. Many actors train at length in specialist programs or colleges to develop these skills. The vast majority of professional actors have undergone extensive training. Actors and actresses will often have many instructors and teachers for a full range of training involving singing, scene-work, audition techniques, and acting for <u>camera</u>.

Three important terms for an actor are : IMAGINATION, CONCENTRATION & OBSERVATION .

Observe people around you. People from different backgrounds and societies. There are lot of different characters around you that you come across in your daily life. Observe their body languages, way of talking and mannerism. This will help you in portraying that particular character in future if you are given one such role. Observe them all with full concentration. After this add on your imagination to the character sketch that you must do as a home work. A good actor will always do the character sketch of the given role or character. Research or observance will help you in this.

Next, when you speak or deliver dialogue, voice should come from your stomach as they say that your chest area should vibrate while you are speaking. This adds base to your voice. A good actor need to have a good diction of language also. This will come through reading habits. Read good scripts, novels, news papers and magazines around you.

IMPROVISATION

Improvisation is a form of acting in which the plot, characters and dialogue of a scene or story are made up in the moment. Actors often improvise their given scene or script by adding on dialogues or moments that are similar to the given scene to them. Such actors are called good actors and they often end up adding beautiful things to the written scenes, making them more wonderful.

CENTER POINT EXERCISE

The most sought after exercise of improvisation is the center point exercise which according to me is the main weapon in an actor's armory who is practicing improvisation. In this exercise, you have to mark a point at a level of your height on a wall or anything available to you. Then imagine that point as any person related to you in any way. It can be your family member, friend, enemy, etc. Talk to that person and imagine his/her reply in your mind that he/she could give you. And finally response to that imagined reply from them. I tell you this exercise would surely open your mind's limits like anything. Your power of thinking would improve.

Now, a great actor training focuses on the whole instrument: voice, mind, heart, and body. While we can't get far without vocal technique, intellectual dexterity, and text-work skills, a strong physical presence is crucial to the professional actor. With that in mind, here are seven movement-based methods all actors should study.

Alexander Technique

This well-known practice applies specialized body-awareness strategies to correct unnecessary tension in actors and non-actors alike. Orator Frederick Matthias Alexander developed the technique in the late 1800s as a way of combating his own vocal problems and quickly discovered that unlearning certain breathing and posture habits was the key to maximizing his own physical functionality. The approach has grown tremendously over the past century; Alexander Technique is taught (and practiced) in training programs across the world, and many actors swear by it as a solution to physical, vocal, and even mental restrictions.

Jacques LecoqTechnique

This renowned actor and teacher used a mix of mime, mask work, and other movement techniques to develop creativity and freedom of expression within his students. L'École Internationale de Théâtre Jacques Lecoq, the Parisian school he founded in 1956, is still one of the preeminent physical training centers in the world, developing artists of all kinds through its two-year conservatory and a variety of specialized workshops. The work is largely improv-based and draws on historical movements like Commedia Dell'arte and clown work as well as Lecoq's famous neutral mask technique and psychological exercises involving elements, colors, and seasons.

Corporeal Mime

According to the great Étienne Decroux, "One of the characteristics of our world is that it is sitting down. Corporeal mime stands up." The famed actor developed the technique as a counterargument to pantomime, using its expressive movements to illustrate abstract concepts—not merely as a placeholder for everyday actions. The technique works inside out as a mode of expression, "making the invisible visible." Physical theaters all over the world use corporeal mime to explore (and illustrate) the inner recesses of human emotion, turning thoughts and feelings into stage-worthy visuals.

Viewpoints

Like corporeal mime, Viewpoints explores human emotion in relation to space, time, and shape, but with specific parameters developed by choreographer Mary Overlie and acting teachers Anne Bogart and Tina Landau. As a theatrical technique, Viewpoints is used to create a story onstage through time (tempo, duration, kinesthetic response, and repetition), space (spatial relationship, topography, architecture, shape, and gesture), and sound (pitch, volume, and timbre). This aesthetically-focused approach is taught to actors and directors alike and has been adopted by major theaters internationally including the renowned <u>SITI company</u> in New York, co-founded by Bogart and Tadashi Suzuki.

The Suzuki Method of Acting

Great Japanese director Tadashi Suzuki came up with this extremely physical regime, which trains actors to work from their core and builds discipline, strength, and focus. The rigorous practice draws on martial arts influences and those of Japanese Noh, Kabuki, and the ancient Greek chorus. Suzuki teaches that acting "begins and ends with the feet"; numerous exercises include controlled (and repetitive) forms of stomping and squatting that create a connected center and bring the body to the brink of exhaustion. The method originated at <u>SCOT (the Suzuki Company of Toga, Japan)</u>, is taught all over the world, and is practiced at the SITI company alongside Bogart's Viewpoints.

The Williamson Technique

Created by actor and teacher Lloyd Williamson as a sort of physical accompaniment to the intellectual training of Sanford Meisner, this technique is known as the "physical process of communication in acting." Drawing on the five senses, Williamson teaches that awareness of sensory stimulation creates experience for the actor; by practicing flexibility and physical connectedness, the actor can begin to create behavior in alignment with that experience. The theory draws on itself; sensory observation creates experience, experience inspires behavior, behavior creates new sensory stimulation, and the cycle continues.

Laban Movement Analysis

As much a language for observing movement as a dedicated acting technique, Rudolf Laban's scientific approach divides movement into four categories: body, effort, shape, and space. Applied to theatrical training, Laban uncovers small nuances behind behavior, examining everything from dramatic movements (throwing oneself across a room) to everyday gestures (flicking a piece of lint off of one's shoulder), and maximizing specificity with every action.

HOW TO WATCH AND ANALYSE A FILM

There's a lot of advice out there about writing film reviews from a critic's perspective, each with varying degrees of advice. Reviews don't need to be complicated. Rather, they need to be honest and encourage discussion. Here are the steps I take from start to finish, when screening films.

STEP 1: BEFORE YOU WATCH THE MOVIE

The hardest part of this first step is going to be avoiding doing too much research or reading other reviews prior to watching the movie (as tempting as it may be.) I find that it's more liberating to the experience to go in with an air of unfamiliarity.

Ideally, when I start on the path of reviewing a film, I will know very little about it—aside from the actors and the director involved. If I'm not familiar with the cast and/or the director, I'll do a little filmography research, but only about their past work if I've never seen it before. Avoiding exposure to the movie can be more difficult than it sounds when it's a popular film—as trailers and marketing run rampant. But if you can avoid watching the trailers and reading about other peoples' opinions prior to watching, you won't have any preconceived judgments and can go in with an unbiased perspective.

Trailers work well to provide some context and tone prior to watching a movie, but they can also be filled with spoilers, which is why I do my best to avoid them when possible. As for reviews, reading about what others think of the movie before watching or writing a review can affect your opinion heavily. And when you're in reviewer mode, you want to be as honest with your own opinion as possible, and not allow any outside voice to alter it. Of course, after the review is finished, I always welcome a discussion with fellow cinephiles to hear and understand what they enjoyed and didn't.

Without being affected by the trailers, marketing, and other reviews before watching a movie, you can really put your best foot forward to creating your authentic opinion and turning that into a movie review people can trust.

STEP 2: WATCHING THE MOVIE

I believe you only need to a see a film once in order to critique a film. Of course, there are those who prefer at least a couple viewings, but from my experience multiple viewings can actually skew your assessment.

What works for me is to watch the movie in its entirety without distractions in order to get a grasp on what the director intended. If you spend your first viewing pausing, playing back, and re-watching segments at a time, you won't get a sense for the way the film was meant to be enjoyed.

I also try not to take many notes while I watch the movie—if you're jotting down a long critique or opinion while watching the movie, you can miss brief, yet vital moments. I will however, write down a word or phrase that stands out so that I can recall scenes or story information that catch my attention and that I deem important. This will help later when I'm constructing my review—for brief summary recaps, breaking down the themes, and reflecting on the direction or acting.

In general, I think of pausing, rewinding, and taking notes as interruptions that will bring you out of the film—literally and emotionally—and that can play a role in how you view a film from a critical standpoint.

STEP 3: AFTER YOU WATCH THE MOVIE

The window of time immediately following the viewing is critical. Since I don't take a lot of notes during the movie, one of the most important aspects of writing a critique is to stay focused and write down all of the things that stood out to me about the film. And since collecting my thoughts after seeing a movie can be chaotic, I need to be sure that I jot down everything that struck my radar as soon as it's over. It's better to get it all down on paper, and then evaluate what's necessary to convey to the reader later. Being precise in your commentary and incorporating specific examples from the movie to back up your opinions is key.

This is where the checklist comes into play. When I write a review, I do my best to cover all aspects of filmmaking that went into creating the final product, including:

Plot: What was the movie about? Was it believable? Interesting? Thought-provoking? How was the climax revealed? How did the setting affect the story?

Themes and Tone: What was the central goal of the movie? Was it made to entertain, educate, or bring awareness to an issue? Was there any strong impression the movie made on you? Did any symbolism come into play?

Acting and Characters: Did you like how the characters were portrayed? Did the acting support the characters, and help them come to life? Did the characters display complex personalities or were they stereotypes? Were there characters that embodied certain archetypes to enhance or diminish the film?

Direction: Did you like how the director chose to tell the story? Was the pacing and speed of the movie too fast or too slow? Was the direction comparable to other movies this director has created? Was the storytelling complex or straightforward? Was there a certain amount of suspense or tension that worked? Did the director create a captivating conflict?

Score: Did the music support the mood of the movie? Was it too distracting or too subtle? Did it add to the production and work well with the script? Were the music queues timed well for the scenes they were supporting?

Cinematography: Were the shots used in a unique way to tell the story? Did the coloring and lighting affect the tone? Was the action coherently shot? How well did the camera move? Were actors or settings framed well?

Production Design: Did the sets feel lived-in and believable to the story or characters? Were the costumes suitable for the characters or story? Did the created environments heighten the atmosphere on camera?

Special Effects: Were the special effects believable? Did they align with the era and tone of the movie? Were the effects overboard or too subtle? Did they integrate well to the purpose of the story?

Editing: Was the editing clean or choppy? Was the flow consistent? What unique effects were used? How were the transitions between scenes?

Pace: Did the movie flow well? Was it too fast or too slow? Was it clearly organized? Did certain scenes drag down the movie?

Dialogue: Were the conversations believable or necessary? Did the dialogue bring context to plot developments? Did the words match the tone of the movie and personality of the characters?

Let's take the special effects as an example. I want to evaluate them based on utility, use within the film, and obviously how well it looks on screen. When I saw Mad Max: Fury Road, I was blown away with all the practical effects and how everything served a purpose to the story. It looked like everything was well crafted and built with love to develop such a brilliantly inspired wasteland.

On the other side of the coin, the Transformers movies, as detailed as the robots look, most of the time while I was watching the movies, I felt like I was watching a jumbled mess of computer animated metal smashing into each other. It didn't look stimulating. You want the special effects to complement the story rather than just being used as a visual device.

STEP 4: WRITING THE REVIEW

After I have all of my thoughts down, I take as much into consideration as I can and then work on the flow. I put a lot of care into the organization of my review, and make sure my thoughts are read in a cohesive manner to help my audience understand where I'm coming from. I prioritize what's most important to include and let the rest go.

Hands down, the most important component to address in a movie review is how it made you feel. Anyone can write a summary of a film or create lists about the highlights. But good reviews should convey to the audience how the movie resonated with you.

If you don't put your voice into your critique, your audience will find it difficult to understand your perspective, connect with you as a reviewer, and most importantly, they may not be able to trust your opinion. And if they don't trust you, they won't come back to read more of your work. And you want your review to provide value to the reader, right?

I want to ensure that my thoughts encourage readers to create a constructive discussion around the film, or help them decide whether or not the movie is for them. And hopefully, the audience will have as much fun reading my review as I did writing it.

CINEMA AND SOCIETY : A RELATIONSHIP

Throughout history, many leaders have used the power of film to help achieve their goals. During WWII, for example, both Hitler and Stalin used movies as propaganda and did so very successfully. Cinema can easily change people's opinions and their outlooks on life. Good films almost always impact the viewer; just how much varies by movie and person. Individually, people are bound to get affected by movies given that a main goal the cinematic art form has is exactly to impact and send a message. There are also numerous ways in which movies affect society and the modern world we live in: some of them negative, some of them positive. Since the cinema industry is so big and because films have become such a big part of our lives, the overall impact and influence that cinema has on our society is immense.

One of the ways in which films affect society is by expanding our knowledge of history and culture.

Some movies are like history lessons to the viewers, since they show real life past events. An example of this is the Academy Award winner for best picture in 2001 "Gladiator". Winner of five Oscars and the nominee for seven more, "Gladiator" is a very well-made production and as close to perfect as few other get. Even though most of the plot in "Gladiator" is fictional, for example the love story and the revenge tale, the film does depict real life past situations. It shows life of gladiators, the political situation of Rome at the time, and the overall state at which the world was. People who have seen "Gladiator" surely gained some knowledge from the film and expanded their current understanding of Roman culture.

Films also describe and explore different cultures around the world. A perfect example of this is the four Oscar nominee "City of God" which takes place in the underground world of Rio de Janeiro. The film surely impacts the viewer since it shows certain situations and truths about life in Rio de Janeiro that most people don't know.

Another huge, and often rather ignored, way that movies affect society is through advertisement of different products.

Often, companies will pay studios to include their products in movies; when so many people watch the production, surely some of them will want to buy the can of Coca-Cola that their favorite character was drinking all throughout. A recent example of this that comes to mind is in the movie "Nerve" starring Dave Franco and Emma Roberts. It's fairly obvious the film is a huge advertisement for Apple. Millions of people went to see that movie; some of them probably had the desire to buy the new Apple product because they saw how well it was working in the hands of the characters. Unlike 'Nerve', however, some productions have found ways to advertise products without shoving them in people's faces. Research has shown that people want to mimic their idols, so productions will often cast famous actors for the sole purpose of advertisement. If someone's favorite actor was AAMIR KHAN, for example, they would subconsciously try to mimic him. If AAMIR KHAN took only one sip from a Coca-Cola can, fans would subconsciously want to buy a Coca-Cola can to be like their favorite actor, even though it's a role they are playing and even though it was, after all, just one sip.

People try to mimic things they've seen in cinema constantly and in numerous different ways. For example, violence in films can be very influential to many young viewers. People may subconsciously try to be like a character they see in a film they very much like, even if that character has wicked intentions. In 2012 in Aurora, Colorado James Holmes killed twelve people and injured seventy others during the midnight projection of "The Dark Knight Rises". James Holmes was a long time superhero fan and especially liked

Batman. Psychologists still aren't sure what exactly provoked him to do the shooting, but one of the theories is that he was enraged by the making of "The Dark Knight Rises" as it defiles his favorite comic book. Another well-known theory is that he was inspired to be like the Joker, the villain of the prequel "The Dark Knight", who wanted to spread chaos and terror through violence. The Joker does not think of ordinary people as real people and James Holmes has said exactly that 'these were not real people'. Although this is a *very* exaggerated example, it's a fact that the violence teenagers all around the world watch in movies makes *them* want to cause violence. For example, in 1971, the same year the classic "A Clockwork Orrange" came out, the crime rate in America rose. It's speculated that some people were influenced by the psychopaths in "A Clockwork Orange" and the awful things they were doing and that affected them in a way that they no longer suppressed their desire to do criminal activity.

But it's not only through violence that people strive to mimic their favorite character and actors. Watching movies that include young people smoking often makes, surprise, surprise, young people want to smoke. Most big movie studios have a tobacco policy in force, which states that PG-13 rated movies must not include smoking or any other use of tobacco in them. That is because the use of tobacco in films affects the teens watching them in a way that they think it's okay to smoke, since the characters they are seeing smoke. However, almost half of all PG-13 film produced by big movie studios do include tobacco use in them and the studios are obligated to pay a fine when that happens.

But there are some positive effects to this mimicking. People are inspired to be like characters they love and that motivates them to work on themselves. When we see someone we really like on screen, we always subconsciously try to be more like them.

Another way in which movies affect our modern world is that they help the economy grow and prosper.

Take, for example, action figures. For every big blockbuster, action figures are created and distributed. Fans buy them for aesthetic and collectible value. Action figures don't have any real application or impact on people's lives, they are just for fun. It doesn't cost a lot for an action figure to be made, they are mostly all made by either plastic, rubber, or both. But since they have such a high collectible value, fans buy them at ridiculously high prices. That way, people bring money into the country, into companies, and into private manufacturers. And it's not only action figures, it's any form of merchandise. Furthermore, the money the theater makes from selling snacks before every screening is 85% of that theater's total profit. Some of that money goes to the country in the form of taxes. Another example of this is simply the tickets sold for projections. Although most of the money goes directly to the studio that has produced the movie, some of it goes to the country. And it's not only direct influence to the country's economy that films have; the industry itself is of huge significance. A lot of people find jobs in the film industry, especially in the US. About 0.1 percent of all people in the USA work in the film industry. Although that may seem like a low percentage, it's actually higher than that of a lot of other fields. So, because of big productions, it's not only that money goes to the country and thus the economy is developed, but private manufacturers and companies prosper and there are more workers in the field.

Films can also both improve and ruin the health of individuals. Studies show that adrenaline junkies love going to horror films since being scared gives them real pleasure. However, most of them don't know that being scared while watching a horror movie increases your heart rate and blood pressure, which can lead to heart attack and even death. For example, a woman died in the theater from heart attack while watching Bollywood horror film "BHOOT". And yes, this is a very specific example, but the principle applies on a smaller scale, too. But of course, films can also give benefits to your health. Comedies help lower your blood pressure and can make your blood vessels dilate. There have been studies that show that 15 minutes of intense laughing while watching a movie have the same effect on the cardiovascular system as exercising.

Perhaps the most influential ways in which films affect society is through giving individual people the opportunity to fantasize and inspiring them about who they want to be.

Although this might sound great, there are, as always, some negative sides to it. Take, for example, the five Oscar nominee "The Wolf of Wall Street". In it, we have the character of Jordan Belfort: a sinister, self-centered, arrogant, and egoistic millionaire. The movie is based on a real story and explores the life of this Wall Street broker. Throughout the movie, there are numerous scenes where we see Jordan spending his money on ridiculous things, doing whatever he wants because he has money, behaving immorally, and actually enjoying his life. By seeing his extravagant lifestyle, viewers may want to be like him.

However, in that particular movie, the character feels absolutely no remorse when it comes to his actions. Jordan feels amazing while spending his money and unlike most other films about greed, there is no lesson to learn from "Wolf of Wall Street". In the end of the movie, Jordan does go to prison, but he states that he feels at peace there. He doesn't learn from his mistakes that much and the movie isn't apologetic about his greed. Someone watching that will see how great it is to be rich and arrogant and might subconsciously think that there are absolutely no downsides to that and may strive towards it.

However, the positives on this one do probably outweigh the negative. Films inspire people to get in the industry and create dreams. Most actors, directors, cinematographers, etc. probably saw some film as children and were thus inspired to create something themselves. This is a very important aspect of how films affect society: they inspire. They inspire individuals to work towards their dreams and inspire them to get into the industry. Not only that, good movies teach valuable lessons. The aim of that is to affect the viewer and to send a message, and so many individuals change their ideals and beliefs because of what they see in films.

Even though it's called 'the seventh art', cinema is surely the most influential art form. Most people don't follow sculpture or architecture and don't get affected by new sculptures or buildings. Movies, however, are everywhere. So many people see movies every day and the film industry is so big and influential. However, movies can affect society in both positive and negative ways. They can help the economy grow, inspire individuals, and expand our basic knowledge of the world around us. Movies can also create violence and bad habits, can make people greedier, and can send a bad message to the public. The effects that films have on society are numerous and two-fold. And as movies are such an impactful art form, big movie studios must be very careful in what they include in their productions, since even the smallest things can affect the viewer. Individuals must be careful about what they take from movies, since even the smallest thing can push them to do something bad or to become someone different. It's fairly clear that movies affect society very much. Not only that, they shape the modern world we live in and help individuals develop. In the big picture, it might be too early to say in what way. All people can currently do is think critically and not allow films to entirely change who they are.

PRODUCTION AND BREAKDOWN

PRODUCTION AND BREAKDOWN

There are basically seven stages of film production.

Development

Pre Production

Production

Principal Photography

Wrap

Post Production

Distribution and Exhibition

Production for a film can be further displayed as the following flow chart. The steps are as follows :

CREW

A Director will look for a script writer with a good script in hand.

Writer will give narration to Director first and then if the director is impressed with the story, both will meet a producer/ funder and narrate the story to him.

After the producer's nod of approval, the pre production of the film starts.

Writer will provide the final draft to the director for shoot.

Director will then hire his direction team (Assistant directors, Associate director, Chief AD).

Hierarchy of the direction team is : (Lower rank – High)

Direction Intern – Director Assistant – Assistant Directors – Chief AD – Creative Director – Associate Director – Director.

This team will now start hiring other members like Makeup team, Art and setting department team, Production team.

Also the Ads team will do the script breakdown, that is to know exactly what is the requirement in each scene in terms of artists, properties, location, Time effect, etc. A genral breakdown procedure/format is as follows :

Script breakdown will help the director to know exactly how many locations are needed in the film's shooting. He would then make a note of all the locations and exact number of scenes as per those locations. Through this he will be able to make a shooting plan that is exactly how many days he would need to shoot the film. This will further help him in making a budget for the film as now he is knowing exactly how many artists for how many days, locations, properties etc he is needing.

Budget breakdown sample is as follows :

budget_percentages.xls_.png

The budget for a film is divided into two categories :

ABOVE THE LINE COSTS including Direction , production , writing departments costs and casting costs.

BELOW THE LINE COSTS includes rest of the costs of the film.

Art director or Production designer will be involved in creating sets for the film with properties to display on set. Production runners will help him in accessing to the properties required for the film. Line producer will help in looking for shoot locations and arranging lodgings and food for the team.

Music director will be hired for songs recording as per the theme of the film. A background music provider will be hired separately as per the scenes in the film and movie genre.

Costume designer will be hired for arranging costumes for actors as per theme and look of the film.

Camera team will be hired with main DOP (Director Of Photography) and his ACs (Assistant Cameramen). First AC is assistant cameraman, Second AC is focus puller and Third AC notes down the Time Code Reading for a particular shot, displaying on display screen of the camera. Time Code is actually the reading of time went for the canning of a particular shot.

Director will sit down with DOP and a storyboard artist for shot divisions of the script. A story board artist will do the story boarding of each scene under the guidance of the director and DOP. This storyboarding will help in understanding how exactly the film would look like on screen.

Several creative inputs can be inserted in the script and when the director actually locks the script that is ready to shoot, it is called the SHOOTING DRAFT.

After the complete pre production has been completed and artists dates are locked, director announces the principal photography dates that is the actual date when the shoot begins.

Now while on shooting, there will be two separate continuity sheets will be maintained. One by the direction team and one by the camera team. The samples are as follows.

05continuity1-ID-aa7165da-3c2d-4c6e-f6a8-92b07dc1063e.png

continuity_form3.jpg

Direction team's continuity sheet has the record of number of takes used for shots and which shot is good or not good to be fit into editing timeline. And camera team's sheet maintains the TIME CODE readings for the same shots. Both the sheets will help the editor to edit the final film.

During the shoots, daily call sheets are also maintained by the direction department for the artists and crew members. This helps in running the shoot smoothly as per the decided schedule. The sample is as follows.

celtx-sample-call-sheet-template.jpg

A producer will provide an EP. An Executive Producer (EP) is a producer who is not involved in the technical aspects of the filmmaking process, but has played a crucial financial or creative role in ensuring that the project goes into production. There may be several Executive Producers on a film who may take the lead role in a number of areas, such as development, financing or production. Executive Producers must be excellent negotiators. They need a keen business sense, and an intimate knowledge of all aspects of film production, financing, marketing and distribution. Executive Producers are responsible for the overall quality control of productions. On some productions the Executive Producer role may be combined with other roles, so that as well as raising the finance they may also be responsible for managing the budget during production. Executive Producers must be able to identify commercial, marketable projects. Executive Producers have overall responsibility for the successful financing and marketing of these projects. During production Executive Producers may be involved in some aspects of scripting, casting, and crewing. Executive Producers often work on a number of projects simultaneously. They are experienced industry practitioners, who have usually worked previously for a number of years in any one of a variety of roles, such as producer, writer, director or script editor. Most have some hands on experience of producing.

Now, during the shoot, some changes are bound to happen in script due to some improvisation in dialogues or scenes by the artists or a sudden location change by the director. Such changes are added in the scripts and after the whole shoot is over, this edited script is termed as Post production draft, on which the editing will happen for the film.

After the editor gives out a final cut version of the film to the director, the same version goes to a master machine for DCP (digital cinema projection) conversion. This process includes all the DI (digital intermediate), color grading processes, making the film fit to be projected on a theatre cinema's screen.

You can use the free/shareware program open DCP so your film can be shown in large format projection rooms. You'll need to use FCPX to export TIFF files.

1. Export your film as a 16-bit TIFF sequence.

2. Use free, open source DCP software to convert the TIFF sequence into JPEG 2000

3. The DCP software then wraps the video (JPEG2000) and audio (WAV) in to MXF files.

4. The final stage is creating the DCP which generates 6 files that will be recognized by a DCP server.

Some Important Terms related to film formats and outputs.

Highest cinema format is .MXF that you display on a movie theatre screen.

.MXF stands for MEDIA XCHANGE FORMAT.

4K format is video resolution having 4000 pixels.

Highest shooting format is IMAX 70 mm cinema format.

FILM DISTRIBUTION

On several occasions, I have been asked by my film students, how the collections of a film are shared among the exhibitor, distributor and producer. Some things to remember before we begin :

Gross Collection: The total amount generated at the ticket counter
(ticket price x number of tickets sold).

Nett Collection: The amount left after the deduction of the entertainment tax. This is the amount that will be available to exhibitors.On an average, entertainment tax across India is assumed to be 40%. Nett collection is not the profit of a film.

Share: The amount an exhibitor forwards to the distributor after deducting their cut (as rent) from the nett.

Although there are various scenarios for who gets what percentage of the nett collections - on average, most exhibitors-distributors-producers follow this breakdown for each film :

Exhibitors' Cut = 45% of nett (single screen and multiplex combined average)
Distributor's Share = 55 % of nett (divided equally with producer after distributor's expenses are deducted).
Producer's Share = 50 % of distributor's profit from nett collections.

So, let's assume a film with a budget of 25 crores costs the distributor 30 crores (with prints and publicity) and does a business of 100 crores nett. The exhibitors' cut is 45 crores, the distributor subtracts 30 crores from his 55 crores and splits the remaining 25 crores 50:50 with the producer (12.5 crores to the distributor and 12.5

crores to producer). The producer sold the film to the distributor for 30 crores and also earned a share of 12.5 crores from nett collections for a total income of 42.5 crores if we subtract the 25 crores cost of production (budget) we get the producer's profit which is = 17.5 crores.

That being said – It's the distributor who assumes the risk of every film. Let's say a film has a budget of 50 crores. Upon completion of the film, the distributor buys the film for 55 crores from the producer and pays for the prints and promotion out of his own pocket. So if he spends 10 crores on prints and promotion, the distributors cost is 65 crores and he needs to earn 65 crores to break even. Following the above mentioned scenario, if this film goes on to collect 100 crores nett, it may be declared a hit, but the distributor loses 10 crores (earning 55 crores of nett collections - 65 crores cost). The exhibitors earns 45 crores nett and the producer earns 5 crores (55 crores from distributor + 0 from the nett collections - 50 crores budget). Because the distributor earned a loss producer doesn't receive any profits from nett collections and yet makes 5 crores profit because he sold it for 5 crores more than the cost of the budget. Similarly, the exhibitor earns a huge income of 45 crores, while the distributor is the only one who earned a loss.

In most cases when a film flops, it's the distributor who loses, the producer and exhibitors are rarely affected. Also, most of the time it's the producers who sell satellite rights, so any money made from satellite rights goes to the producer and the distributor doesn't get a penny from it.

So, again in the above scenario if the satellite rights of the film are sold for 25 crores, the producer earns 30 crores (55 crores from distributor + 25 crores Satellite - 50 crores budget), while the distributor loses 10 crores.

In some cases, the distributor owns the satellite rights of the film, in that scenario, our distributor would've earned 15 crores profit (earning 55 crores from theatrical release + 25 crores from satellite rights - 65 crores cost).

Now let's put our formula to work on some popular BOLLYWOOD hits and see what happens.

Dabangg – at a cost of 40 crores – had collected 140 crores nett. **Arbaaz Khan** (producer) kept some of the distribution territories of the film, so the distribution cost was approximately 30 crores for the territories the distributor held.

Out of the 140 crores nett:
Exhibitors' cut = 63 crores (45%)

Distributor's share = 77 crores (55%) – 30 crores cost = 47 crores/2 = 23.5 crores **profit**
Producer's share = 50% of 47 crores = 23.5 crores + 30 crores (sale to distributor) + 20 crores (revenue from self-distribution) + 10 crores (satellite rights) - 40 crores (budget) = 43.5 crores**profit**

Another recent hit, **3 idiots** was sold for 35 crores. It collected 202 crores nett.
Exhibitors' cut = 91 crores
Distributor's share = 111 crores - 40 crores cost = 71 crores/2 = 35.5 crores **profit**
Producer's share = 35.5 crores + 35 crores (sale to distributor) + 35 crores (satellite rights) – 30 crores (budget) = 75.5 crores **profit**

The Tamil blockbuster **Enthiran**, was sold for 160 crores. **Enthiran** was being made out to be one of the biggest hits ever. But the numbers tell a different story. The first weeks collections of **Enthiran** were 105 crores nett (probably because the average ticket price was Rs. 500, while the average ticket price of **Dabangg** and **3 idiots**were Rs. 100). The total nett collections for **Enthiran** for week 1 and 2 were approximately 125 crores nett. At most the life time business of **Enthiran** will be 150 crores nett.

This means:
Exhibitors' cut = 67.5 crores
Distributor's Share = 82.5 Crores - 170 crores cost = -87.5 crores **loss**
Producer's share = 0 crores (from nett collections) + 160 crores (from distributor) – 150 crores (budget) = 10 crores **profit**

So, when a distributor makes a loss of 87.5 crores, it's hardly correct to declare the film a hit. In order for **Enthiran** to be declared a hit, it had to collect over 310 crores nett. It needed to collect 310 crores nett just for the distributor to break even. This is where Indian filmmakers/ distributors make their mistakes.

If a film costs 170 crores it has to earn twice that amount in order for the distributor to make a profit and since no film has ever done that much business in India, it boggles the mind to think how filmmakers can make films at such high budgets. Indian films should not be made for more than 30-35 crores if they intend to make a substantial profit for their distributors and producers. At budgets over 100 crores the only one with any hope of making money is the exhibitor, everyone else loses out.

In the end, I would like to conclude that Film making is an intense complex process that requires sheer determination and concentration. It is a team work at the end of the day. A good director will always have a clear picture in his mind of what he is shooting exactly. Go ahead, lift a good quality camera, pick a good script and start shooting now!

Quotes For All Film Enthusiasts

1. Its far better to shoot a good film rather than a good looking film.

2. Everything that can be written, can be filmed too! Dont hesitate ever to trust yourself.

3. There can never be a zero budget film, Its always a small budget film.

4. If you have a story, just take a camera and start shooting. Otherwise time is passing by and it won't stop ever to give you chance again.

5. And last but not the least, always try becoming a good human first. Remember, its always a team work to make a film and that team will only work for you whole heartedly if you are a genuine person.